BENTLEY, FIFTY YEARS OF THE MARQUE

This book is dedicated to everyone for whom the marque Bentley means more than just mere transportation, and is intended as a tribute to the man whose motors have given such pleasure to so many for fifty years, products which have become a legend within the lifetime of their creator W. O. Bentley.

WALTER OWEN BENTLEY, M.B.E.

July, 1963

Commissioned by members of the Bentley Drivers Club. Painted by William Dring, R.A., R.W.S.

BENTLEY

FIFTY YEARS OF THE MARQUE

JOHNNIE GREEN

DALTON WATSON LTD
LONDON

First Published 1969
Reprinted 1973
Revised 1974
Reprinted 1978

ISBN 901564 00 1

© DALTON WATSON LTD.
Process Engravings by Star Illustration Works Ltd.
Printed in England by the Lavenham Press Ltd.
for the publishers
DALTON WATSON LTD.
76 Wardour Street, London W1V 4AN

Distributed in the U.S.A. by
MOTORBOOKS INTERNATIONAL
3501 Hennepin Avenue South
Minneapolis
Minnesota 55408

An appreciation

It is given to few to be blessed with the tenacity of purpose necessary to produce a work of this nature. One possessed of this quality, and at the same time an encyclopaedic knowledge of his subject, is a rarity indeed.

That Johnnie Green is so endowed and that his subject should be Bentleys is our good fortune, for this addition to the lore of the marque is unique. Not only will it be accepted as the standard work of reference on Bentley coachwork, but it will provide many hours of pleasurable browsing, and will bear returning to again and again. Many of the Bentleys pictured in this book are still in existence in the hands of loving owners, and serve as a living testimony to a dying craft.

I commend you to sit back and relish this welcome newcomer to your library of motoring classics.

Stanley Sedgwick, *President*

Cobham, Surrey, England
March, 1969

BENTLEY DRIVERS CLUB

Introduction

Even before my brother-in-law, Lawrence Dalton, had finished his book, "Those Elegant Rolls-Royce", he was asking when I was going to produce the work on Bentleys. Frankly I felt that practically everything had already been said by more able and far better informed people about this famous marque, but when it became fully appreciated that 1969 would see the celebration of 50 years of Bentleys, my natural enthusiasm for these motors, stemming from their glorious Le Mans days, prompted me to weaken, and undertake to try and provide a pictorial review of all the different Bentley models over this period in the history of motoring. This project was considerably influenced and encouraged by the Bentley Drivers Club, on whose committee I have had the privilege of sitting for some 20 years, and therefore could not very easily disregard the wishes of their president, and my close friend, Stanley Sedgwick.

There will be few technicalities in this book, partly because I am ill equipped for such work, but mainly because all these points have been thoroughly dealt with in "The Technical Facts of the Vintage Bentley", and in the works manuals, and new supplement now planned for the Derby-built cars.

Rather will it be a survey of the different coachwork fitted over these 50 years to the various models of Bentley, and while no treatise on this make could be envisaged without reference to their racing successes (and the author is such an admirer of the team cars that the reader may be assured nearly every one of these is included) it is not intended that a full survey of their competition history should appear, as this subject has already been dealt with in masterly fashion by Darell Berthon ("Racing History of the Bentley"), the executive vice-president of the B.D.C. (Bentley Drivers Club—we might as well adopt these initials now, as inevitably they will recur throughout this book), for without Darell's and Barbara Gunstone's unstinted co-operation, this book would not have been feasible.

Innumerable club members have generously contributed from their own private records, and a separate acknowledgments section will endeavour to give credit for this much valued help, but this subject cannot be dismissed without mention of Harry Fergusson-Wood and John Cochrane, both then with Jack Barclay's, for their enormous help in furnishing material on the post-vintage cars, and to an employee of the old Bentley Company, A. F. Rivers Fletcher, for so kindly placing at my disposal so many of the old company's official photographs taken in the late 20's.

Despite some misgivings as to the possible reception and popularity of the book, I cannot for one moment pretend I haven't enjoyed this challenge, for my heart has been lost more thoroughly to this make of car than any other for over 40 years, but as so many of the captions rely upon my memory and personal acquaintance with these motors, I trust if any inaccuracies exist, they will be forgiven as over-exuberance, rather than the intention ever to mislead.

In this connection, the present ownership of numerous cars is given, but I can only fall back upon the last recorded information available, and changes may in some instances have taken place since. With the considerable amount of material which has been available, severe restraint has had to be exercised in selecting, where possible, only the better photographs and trying to avoid too much repetition, and here undoubtedly arises the cue for dealing with the matter of coachwork by Messrs. Vanden Plas (England) 1923 Ltd.

If the reader may criticise some lack of variety in bodies shown, particularly on the 3 Litre chassis, perhaps not every Bentley follower may be aware of the extraordinarily high percentage of Vanden Plas tourers produced for the earlier cars. An interesting day spent with E. Rowland Fox of Vanden Plas unearthed fascinating details of early deliveries and owners' names. That some thousand-odd bodies were mounted on the total production of 3,031 vintage Bentleys made between 1919 and 1931 by this concern may alone account for the popular belief that most Bentleys are painted green and fitted with an open fabric covered four-seater tourer, with two small doors, one nearside front and one offside rear, and in my own opinion no more perfectly proportioned or aesthetically correct style ever found its way on to any chassis frame of that period, but it does restrict one's choice and consequently dictates to a large extent the form in which this publication appears.

Every endeavour has been made to find new photographs not previously published in book form, and it is thought some 70 per cent of those appearing, do so for the first time, even if occasionally both car or driver may be familiar, you simply cannot keep a good dog down.

The layout chosen has been by each model as it has appeared in sequence, from the 3 Litre of 1919 to the current "T" series, and with the former, that no fewer than five of the 14 models only produced on the 9 ft. wheelbase 100 m.p.h. chassis appear, occurs purely because, as far as I know, each of these cars had entirely different individual coachwork, and that is just what we wanted.

During those twelve or so eventful years between 1919 and 1931, a legend was created, mainly brought about by the simple expedient of one man just producing the best he knew how, W.O., still amazed to this day by the fame his cars have achieved.

After each era of the marque, the Vintage years (1919–1931), the Derby-built cars of 1933–1940, and the post-war Crewe motors, appears a chapter devoted to the more sporting activities of the particular period under review, as throughout the development of Bentleys, sportsmen have found their thoroughbred construction ideal for modification for competitive purposes, and it has been this enduring ruggedness and emphasis upon reliability which has enabled four generations to enjoy a form of motoring which will never be forgotten by those who have been fortunate enough to have experienced it.

J.G.

Acknowledgements

The author would like to record his most sincere appreciation for the kind assistance given by the following, whose photographs appear on the pages indicated against their names, and also to thank many other Bentley enthusiasts who submitted numerous contributions, which in some cases due to duplication, were not reproduced.

Without this unstinted co-operation this publication would not have been possible.

G. Albertini, Esq., 23, 139; N. Allen, Esq., 130; J. Scott Appleby, Esq., 111; R. S. Atherton, Esq., 134; H. Austin Clarke, Esq., (Jnr.), 70; The Autocar, 150; Jack Barclay Ltd., 81, 82, 89, 115, 118, 119, 125, 128, 129, 136, 170, 171, 174, 175, 176, 177, 182, 183, 185, 187, 188, 189, 190, 191, 193, 195, 196, 198, 199, 200, 201, 202, 203, 206, 207, 208, 209, 210, 211, 215, 216, 217, 219, 221, 222, 223, 224, 227, 233, 245, 246, 247, 248, 250, 251, 252, 253, 254, 256, 257, 258, 260, 261, 263, 264, 265, 268, 271, 272, 273, 275, 276, 278, 279; O. Batten, Esq., 128; The Bentley Drivers' Club, 18, 19, 20, 21, 22, 23, 24, 25, 27, 28, 30, 31, 32, 34, 35, 36, 37, 38, 39, 40, 42, 43, 44, 46, 47, 52, 55, 57, 58, 59, 64, 68, 69, 71, 72, 73, 76, 85, 86, 87, 88, 89, 90, 91, 92, 93, 94, 95, 96, 97, 100, 101, 103, 105, 106, 107, 108, 110, 114, 116, 117, 120, 121, 123, 124, 125, 126, 128, 130, 131, 132, 133, 134, 135, 138, 139, 140, 141, 142, 143, 144, 146, 147, 148, 149, 150, 152, 153, 154, 155, 156, 157, 158, 159, 160, 163, 168, 172, 178, 180, 192, 196, 198, 201, 202, 213, 214, 216, 227, 228, 235, 238, 239, 240, 241, 242, 246, 266, 282, 283, 284, 285, 286; Bentley Motors (1931) Ltd., 162, 163, 164, 165, 166, 167, 168, 169, 170, 173, 177, 178, 180, 181, 182, 185, 186, 188, 189, 191, 193, 194, 198, 205, 206, 207, 212, 224, 226, 236, 244, 250, 251, 252, 253, 255, 256, 258, 261, 262, 264, 265, 266, 270, 274, 276, 279, 280; P. Blake, Esq., 66; R. Broster, Esq., 225; B. Brown, Esq., 27, 37, 88, 132, 178, 180, 229, 234, 235; M. Ellman Brown, Esq., 232, 234, 235; W. J. Chapman, Esq., 86; J. Coates, Esq., 67; R. W. Colton, Esq., 98; W. Cronckhite, Esq., 204; F. Dale, Esq., and Stepsons, 72, 195, 196, 202, 246, 258; H. Fergusson-Wood, Esq., 29, 74, 75; H. F. Fry, Esq., of F.L.M. Panelcraft Ltd., 23, 206, 213; M. H. N. Haggitt, Esq., 33; R. Hames, Esq., 84; The Harrah Automobile Museum, 114; H. Hinchcliffe, Esq., 163, 165, 167, 168, 170, 172, 174, 179, 181, 183, 184, 187, 189, 195, 203, 204, 207, 216, 219, 221, 223, 226, 230, 241, 254, 257, 258, 259; D. L. P. Humfrey, Esq., 66; John im Thurn, Esq., 146; H. Jones, Esq., 220; W. D. S. Lake, Esq., 62; S. V. Lipscombe, Esq., 48; R. G. McLeod, Esq., 250, 265, 275; J. A. MacHarg, Esq., 132; D. T. Manley, Esq., 184; The Manx Motor Museum, 59; W. Möller, Esq., 218; B. Morgan, Esq., 67; J. Nethercutt, Esq., 249; W. Nicholson, Esq., 64; T. E. Reich, Esq., 131, 187, 194, 223, 230; O. F. Rivers, Esq., 45, 47, 80, 82, 186, 191, 199, 201, 208, 249, 252, 262, 263, 269; A. F. Rivers Fletcher, Esq., 21, 26, 46, 47, 48, 49, 51, 52, 54, 55, 56, 59, 60, 61, 62, 63, 65, 68, 69, 78, 79, 81, 83, 87, 90, 102, 103, 104, 110, 112, 113, 125, 127, 135, 145, 228; W. J. D. Roberts, Esq., 192; B. M. Russ-Turner, Esq., 101, 242; Saga Services Ltd., 67; C. B. D. Sargeant, Esq., 192; D. Scott-Moncrieff, Esq., 52,

Contents

CHAPTER ONE

3 LITRE

Every Bentley addict already knows the early history of this immortal machine whose first prototype engine burst into life noisily in a mews off Baker Street in 1919. The author has a very soft spot for this model, because the last one produced by the old company gave him twelve years of blissful motoring, the memory of which will live for ever, and this, W.O.'s first motor car creation, must have provided an introduction to the real thing for more enthusiasts than any other car.

The prototype engine had a water pump driven from one side of the front cross-shafts and a single magneto on the opposite side. This was changed to twin magnetos, one on either side and skew gears driving the water impeller which nestled into the V of that classic radiator.

Dry sump lubrication was envisaged for the original layout, but an almost separate container beneath the main crankcase became practice on the production models between 1921 and 1926. This was later replaced by the big sump design of 1926 to 1929, which was also used on the four RC series chassis made up from spares by the Rolls-Royce company after their takeover.

A separate book could be written on their performance figures, but whether Standard (Blue Label if I dare use such an unofficial descriptive term) or the Speed Model (and Red Labels will be found engraved on the heart of many a 3 litre owner) every 3 if left unspoilt by non-original tyre sizes gave delightful handling characteristics. Maximum speeds ranged from approximately 70 m.p.h. if too heavily encumbered by limousine coachwork, to a genuine 100 m.p.h. from the fourteen 9 ft. wheelbase editions, where recourse to 3.53 to 1 rear axles was made, and when several miles of unencumbered Route Nationale could be assured.

The 3 Litre provided instant success for the marque Bentley and its throbbing 4 cylinder beat still remains an inspiration today.

Brief Specification: 80 mm. bore × 149 mm. stroke, 2,996 c.c.
4 cylinder, single overhead camshaft engine.
Wheelbase: 9ft.; 9ft. 9½in. and 10ft. 10in.
Track: 4ft. 8in.

Number of cars made: 10ft. 10in. wheelbase   779
9ft. 9½in. wheelbase   831
9ft.   wheelbase   14
Total   1,624

Above, the Man and the Machine. No explanation for the capital letters is necessary to Bentley addicts. W. O. Bentley in the first experimental 3 Litre in January 1920, when tested by the Autocar and reported on by S. C. H. (Sammy) Davis.

Below, A. F. C. Hillstead's (Sales Manager for Bentleys) demonstration model, with production engine No. 1 in chassis No. 5, registration number MD 9756, with coachwork by Ewarts of geyser fame, ordered as a fourth body identical to those fitted to the three T.T. cars. The horizontally mounted spare wheel may be seen protruding from the tail. The carrosserie was finished in scratched, then varnished aluminium, with red mudguards.

Above, "as it was in the beginning." The first experimental 3 Litre engine of 1919, photographed in its test bed in a Baker Street mews, before being lowered through a trap door, which still exists, to the chassis waiting below, in the coachbuilding premises of Messrs J. H. Easter and Son, where pilgrims are welcomed.

Below, the production unit of 1921-1926 will be seen to differ from the engine above, with its almost separate divided sump, twin magnetos and forward driven water pump replacing the earlier single mag' and transverse water impellor. The version shown here is the twin sloper SU carburettor speed model of 1924/26, the alternative to the single 5 jet Smiths carburettor fitted to the standard edition.

Touring as in the mid 20's, the Auster rear screen, fitted to a Gurney Nutting body, is typical of that era of motoring. Chassis number 930, registration number CR 9914, seen here in the U.S.A. in the ownership of R. W. Fisher, Esq.

Listed as a light tourer model, chassis number AP317, registration number MK 2522 fitted with coachwork by Vanden Plas, and owned by W. F. Price, Esq.

An original though unusual touring version by Vanden Plas, fitted to speed model chassis number ML1519, and registered YT 6067, for several years a consistent concours winner, and now owned by The Lord Cranworth.

Not all Vanden Plas tourers were four seaters. This clover leaf three passenger car permitted all members to share the hood's protection. Fitted to a speed model chassis, it cost its original owner, Mrs. Jacobsen, £1,300 in 1927.

The standard 10ft. 10in. wheelbase chassis fitted with (right first time) a Vanden Plas touring body, afforded roomy accommodation for up to five people.

One of the fourteen 100 m.p.h. 9 ft. wheelbase models. This one chassis number 1126 carrying its guarantee date from 16th May 1925 emigrated to Australia. Here she is "down under" about to take the Talberg Hill record.

This early (1923) 3 Litre bears a very unusual pointed tail body by Vanden Plas with polished wooden decking.

Though the upper car, with coachwork by Cole and Shuttleworth fitted to chassis number LT1587 and registered YR 8111, carries the familiar 100 m.p.h. model radiator, not all these rare cars were so equipped, and the ex-Woolf Barnato motor, originally bodied by Jarvis, as raced at Brooklands, shewn below, wears the normal 3 Litre shaped matrix. This car was skilfully rebuilt by F. L. M. Panelcraft for Gerry Albertini, Esq., chassis number 1106 and registered PE 3200, and now owned by W. D. S. Lake, Esq.

Above, the 2-seater coachwork fitted to this early chassis, number 424, registered KR2564, is reputed to be by Boon and Porter (then the distributors for that amusing little French sports car The Amilcar). The front wheel brakes are a later addition, and this motor now resides in the U.S.A.

Below, if not aesthetically beautiful, the body fitted to this very early chassis, number 19, was specially executed by Gairns of Edinburgh to the design of T. Davidson, Esq., who kept her for over thirty years, before passing to her present owner W. P. Dale, Esq., here seen at Ferodo's, welcomed by their P.R.O., Mr. Jupe, himself the keen owner of a Speed Six.

During the '30's several Bentleys were fitted with replacement bodies, surplus new stock from well known large manufacturers. Messrs Cooper of Putney were exponents of such conversions, and the fixed head coupé at the top, registration YP 41, will be recognizable to many as deriving from a Morris Major, the larger Isis version finding its way on to the 4½ Litre chassis.

This chassis number TN1554, registered RM 3927, originally fitted with a Freestone and Webb Weymann saloon, has since been fitted with a sports tourer destined for the Austin 12/6, and then listed as an alternative to their standard models, at least six 3 Litres were so converted.

The bottom car depicted here is a "one-off" Malayan construction by Japanese labour, and the body, if a little Bugattish in line, has nevertheless been very neatly executed.

No! Not this time, but by Coopers, and differing around the scuttle line and body cut away from the more familiar V.D.P. version. Here seen in the ownership of Guy Shoosmith, Esq., who installed a 4½ litre engine, she has since departed to the U.S.A. where she is now owned by R. Johnson, Esq.

Below, although apparently here painted black, this 1927 speed model has throughout most of her life been finished in beige with green mudguards. Chassis number AX1674, and registered YH 2808, she is at present owned by C. K. W. Schellenberg, Esq., and her Vanden Plas body is still in its original state.

William Arnold was responsible for this all weather body fitted to a standard chassis, registration number CA 6600 and here shown at the first Goodwood Pageant in 1964, in the ownership of B. W. Payne, Esq.

Doctor's Coupé was a designation often applied to this form of coachwork, though Mulliners, who were responsible for this edition, fitted to chassis number 1093, registered YK 3114, describe it as a Cabriolet Coupé, owned by D. W. Vaughan, Esq.

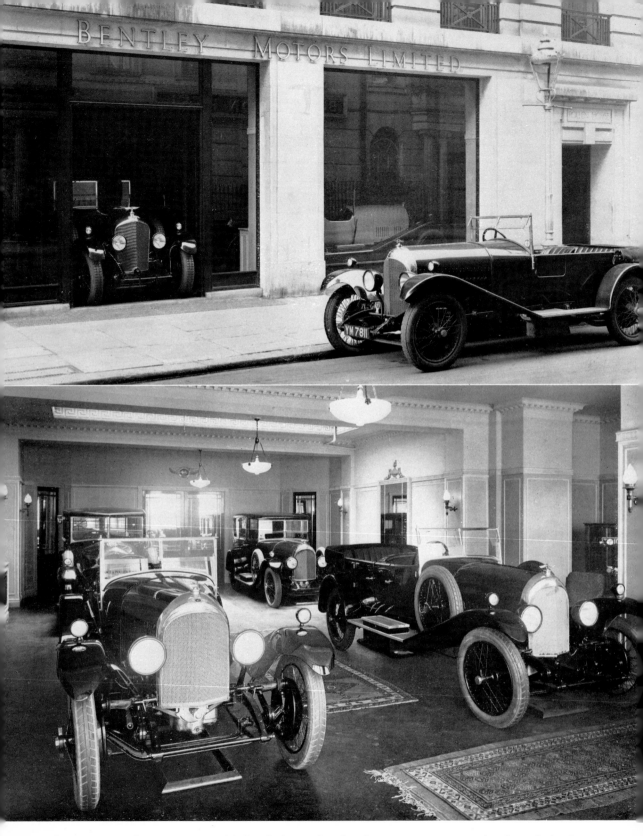

Pollen House, Cork Street, circa 1926, Bentley's new London showrooms, seen emerging through the doorway is a very early Big Six, and below an interior shot of these premises.

The White City Show of 1921, in the upper picture one of the earliest Gurney Nutting saloons fitted to a 3 Litre, and below the Gurney Nutting stand at the Olympia Show of 1925.

Devotees of Kensington Gardens rallies will recognise G. W. Daniels's superb rebuild to Champion standards of a Gurney Nutting Landaulette fitted to chassis number 762 and registered P D 3211.

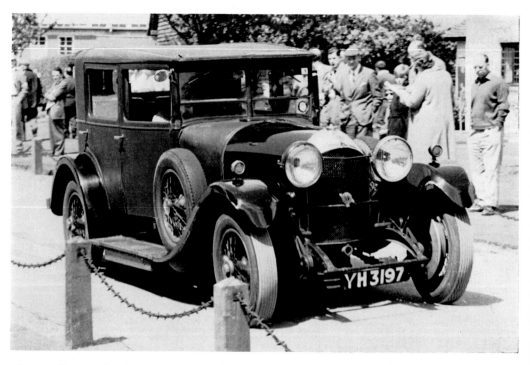

Also of Gurney Nutting construction is this Weymann fabric saloon fitted to chassis number AX1656 registered YH 3197 on 27th May, 1927, now owned by R. L. Rolt, Esq.

Thought to be unique, and possibly by Jarvis, the front valence treatment is most unusual, and the owner seems to have specified hand pressure petrol feed with his well stocked instrument panel.

Here Vanden Plas have adopted a nautical line in this boat tailed three seater fitted to chassis number 1207 and registered YP 8041 on 31st March, 1926, now owned by Lawrence McCann, Esq., of Illinois.

This bumble tail two seater, registration number XM 4277 on chassis number 137, guarantee date 20th August 1922, has the author baffled as to the name of the coachbuilder, the lines of which closely resemble those of the body later fitted to "Old Number Seven" before she was written off round a telegraph post in about 1936.

Wearing her 1925 "Le Mans" racing number and registered M D 7187. This was the car driven by Clement and Duff, in that year, when petrol consumption calculations were upset by the added wind resistance from the raised hoods decreed by the regulations. No. 9 retired due to a fire after 64 laps.

BENTLEY 3 LITRE 4 SEATER SPEED MODEL
COACHWORK BY VANDEN PLAS (ENGLAND) 1923 LTD.

Though bearing close resemblance to the "Le Mans" car above, this Vanden Plas tourer has the more familiar rear mounted spare wheel and standard 11-gallon petrol tank.

The last 3 Litre produced by the old company, chassis number DN1741, registered UV 7549 (28th August, 1929) competing at an early post-war V.S.C.C. Bisley meeting. Despite over 12 years idyllic ownership, the author only recently discovered the body to be by Wylder.

Competing "down under" in the International Rally at Teretonga Park, New Zealand, M. H. N. Haggitt in his self-constructed four-seater tourer.

A rare Jarvis bodied boat tail
2 seater, displaying the ship-like
ventilator cowls on the scuttle top,
typical of this style of coachwork,
on chassis number 1050,
registered YK 2943 and owned
by G. H. Ryley, Esq.

One of the few H. M. Bentley
and Partner rebuilds executed in
about 1935 on 3, 4½ and Speed
Six chassis. This one was probably
the only hybrid 3/4½ edition, and
was supplied to the late J. G. Fry,
Esq., registered DLR 8. This car
was fitted with a central gear
lever, and after tuning by
Robin Jackson, Esq., achieved
108 m.p.h.

Miss Elizabeth Nagle (now
Mrs. Turnbull) in her well-known
boat tail 3 seater by H. J.
Mulliner, their only body of this
pattern made for a Bentley, here
seen competing in the Australian
International Rally. A heavy
crankshaft 4½ Litre engine
is now fitted to this car, registration number XY 196.

Several vintage Bentleys were re-bodied with new contemporary coachwork in the 30's, though few possessing as pleasing lines as this saloon by Coachcraft Ltd., on chassis number 784. This was to the design and order of W. H. Shortt, Esq., in 1935, and then fitted with an E.N.V. preselector gearbox, an anachronism since removed.

This Freestone and Webb fabric Weymann saloon is mounted on chassis number 1194 and registered YL 4117. She belongs to G. E. Spears, Esq.

Specially made for the Scottish Motor Show, this Sedanca-de-Ville is by Hoopers.

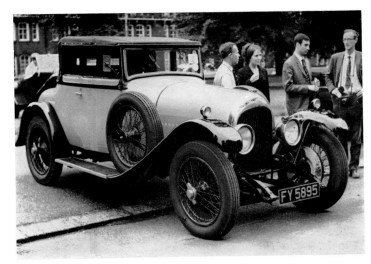

Noel Pizey's unique drop head coupé by Carbodies of Coventry on short standard chassis, number 317, and registered FY 5895, at the 1968 Kensington Gardens Rally.

Another delightful period piece, by Salmons, this coupé was removed from another 3 Litre, to be fitted to chassis number 242, and registered KU 2274, now in the possession of M. R. B. Way, Esq.

This example is by Freestone and Webb finished in deep green with gold and red lining, more reminiscent of an earlier era, registered OP 4536, as presented by the late Warren E. Lovesy, Esq.

Bentleys themselves in about 1935 rebuilt a few 3 Litres, endowing them with new bodies, this drop head coupé by Corsica, is on long chassis number SR1405, registered WW 2429, then priced by the works at £525, and now owned by Dr. D. P. King.

Still retaining several of her original Park Ward features, this early chassis number 92 owned by H. Haneborg, Esq., has had her Cabriolet body modernised with lowered V screen, and the rear quarter lights dispensed with, to accommodate the new recessed hood arrangement.

Italian craftsmen were responsible for this body by Viotti of Turin, fitted to chassis number 650 and registered XU 5160. Owner – R. L. Atwell, Esq., of Texas.

This Vanden Plas tourer was successfully raced by Eric Forest Greene in the Argentine, and now owned by J. B. Ward, Esq. Chassis number BL1619 and registered in U.K. as MG 1280.

Long chassis number NR503 registered YM 8765 is credited with coachwork by Vickers. Her present engine LM1341 is from "Old Number 7", hero of the 1927 White Horse crash. Owner J. W. Alington, Esq.

Early birds! On the left, Stuart Cranfield's reconstituted Indianapolis car of 1922, original chassis number 94, and registered ME 4976, now in the museum of that famous American race centre, here motoring alongside C. A. Wadsworth's 1922 model, chassis number 84, registration number XL 4766, with coachwork by Lawton Goodman, a car rebuilt by its enthusiastic owner to remarkably authentic 1921 specification, and the third of this trio at the first big Goodwood Pageant in 1964 is G. E. Baughan's Vanden Plas tourer, chassis number 452, registered XR 6056 which acquired its 5-year guarantee date on 19th January, 1924.

CHAPTER TWO

6½ LITRE

By 1924, with only four years production of the 3 Litre model, customers were already lumbering this long-suffering chassis with bodies far in excess of the weight intended by the designer. W.O. was not one to see a fine machine abused, so work commenced on a bigger six cylinder motor, where smoothness and quietness would be in keeping with the luxury limousine coachwork insisted upon by the rapidly expanding clientele.

In 1925 the well developed prototype was returning across France on test, when a chance encounter with the "New Phantom" Rolls-Royce, also on trials, led to an unexpected and so closely contested race, that Bentley's decided to increase the capacity of the then 4½ Litre 6 cylinder unit to the 6,597 c.c. size, in which form it remained throughout its life from 1926 to 1930.

The 6½ Litre Big Six still employing a single Smith's 5 jet carburettor was, in late 1928, supplemented by the Speed Six version. This was recognizable externally by parallel sides to its impressive radiator, the Standard 6½ having a tapering radiator, not dissimilar in shape to that used on the 100 m.p.h. 3 Litre cars. Mechanically the main changes were a higher compression ratio and twin S.U. carburettors.

The last chassis of the Speed Six series were the two 1930 Le Mans cars, which went on to cover themselves in glory and provided a degree of reliability remarkable even by Bentley standards.

That the Speed Six was W.O.'s favourite among his illustrious machines, can readily be understood by anyone who has driven any distance to the accompaniment of the gentle roar and almost turbine-like never ending surge of power from beneath that long slim bonnet.

Brief Specification: 100 mm. bore × 140 mm. stroke, 6597 c.c.
6 cylinder, coupling rod driven single overhead camshaft engine.

Wheelbases: Standard 6½	11ft., 12ft 1¼in., and 12ft. 7¼in.	
Speed Six	11ft. 8½in. and 12ft. 8½in.	
Le Mans cars	11ft.	

Track: 4ft. 8in.

Number of cars made:		
Standard 6½	373	
Speed Six	171	
Total	544	

While still of only 4½ litre capacity, the first experimental Big Six, in France on test in 1925. Wearing a disguised radiator, and registered as "The Sun", there is good evidence shown here of the tyre problems then experienced.

In the photograph below the engine is thought to have already been increased to the 6597 c.c. which remained the size of the 6½ throughout its five-year life.

The 6½ Litre production line at Cricklewood, where most chassis appear to be Speed Sixes, awaiting their radiators, and on the left one ready for test.

Below we have Douglas Symond's shortened 10ft. 10in. wheelbase version of a "Le Mans" model (his garage length decreed that dimension) before receiving her VDP style coachwork. The cylindrical oil catchers around the propeller shaft are typical of this perfectionist. The rounded lid of a 'D' type gear box will be noted.

"They don't make 'em like it now." A Harrison limousine on chassis number WB2562, registered YF 9093, while owned by Philip Blake, Esq., before a crash necessitated replacement with a Freestone and Webb coupé body.

Below, Lt. Col. Hamilton's Hooper saloon as in 1927, fitted to chassis number KD2112 and registered YT 56.

An H. J. Mulliner Weymann saloon fitted to chassis number FR2645 and registered UV 1926.

W. O. Bentley's own personal 3 Litre, seen here in the rural surroundings of Winchester Cathedral in about 1922, fitted with an all weather body. Registration number BM 9771.

Two almost identical bodies to this two seater were apparently produced, the one owned by Doctor Taylor has been attributed to Corsica, whereas it is felt Messrs. Vanden Plas were responsible for that shown here.

We know the coupé coachwork on chassis number FR2647 registration number VW 566 to be by Mulliners, and this Speed Six model acquired her guarantee on 18th September, 1929.

Messrs. Hoopers described this special Scottish Motor Show exhibit as a 2/4 seater Cabriolet, which is mounted on the standard 6½ Litre chassis circa 1927.

H. J. Mulliner described this as a Simplex Coupé, she cost her original owner, Mrs. Cholmondeley, £2,025 in September, 1926, and is now owned by K. A. White, Esq., in South Africa.

This slightly different line and sloping windscreen seemingly by B. Napoleon, was devised by Vanden Plas for the 1929 Olympia Motor Show, on what appears to be a short chassis Speed Six, which apart from the "Le Mans" cars and one other, usually had an 11ft. 8½in. wheelbase.

Long Distance Tourer was Vanden Plas's appellation for S. V. Lipscombe's 6½, registration number G 1117. The hand brake arrangement is unusual.

The swept down line with low body sides, and small rear trunk impart a rakish line to this H. J. Mulliner tourer which cost £1,975 complete, when new.

This was Vanden Plas's standard long distance tourer on the Speed Six chassis. The spare wheel was semi-recessed into the tail in similar fashion to the 1928 Bob Tail "Le Mans" cars, and the rear deck hinges forward to allow access to the tonneau.

Once owned by the Marquis of Dufferin and Ava, this beautifully proportioned coupé by the Mayfair Carriage Co. on chassis number LR2780, has had the front mudguards modified from the original full length sweeping form. The coachwork is unusual in being of 2/4/6 seating capacity.

The stainless steel waistband as shown in this drop head coupé, was a feature often adopted by H. J. Mulliner on their coachwork, here mounted on Speed Six chassis.

Park Ward used the term Salamanca to describe this all weather bodywork, which could be used in sedanca de ville position or, by releasing the central pillars, fully open state.

Chassis number LB2328 wears a close coupled saloon on Weymann principles by Victor Broom, one-time coachbuilders of Camden Town in North London.
And below, a sedanca de ville by Thrupp and Maberly on chassis number KF2380, and registered XV 9488 with guarantee date from 30th January, 1929.

We are open to any suggestions on the coachwork identity of these two machines, the upper fabric saloon bears the hall-marks of both Gurney Nutting and Freestone and Webb, while the drop head coupé in the lower picture would appear to have some Hoyle leanings.

The Hon. James Bruce's very practicable drop head coupé by H. J. Mulliner on a Speed Six, whose registration number SMX 158 is thought to stem from her days with the Austin family.

A delightful coupé by Gurney Nutting, with distinctive float type running boards on chassis number KR2699 and registered UW 31, as used in the City of London Lord Mayor's Show to lead an early motor cavalcade.

Gill were responsible for this all weather body under patent by "Hibbard and Darrin" of Paris. Chassis number NH2750, registered GN 5268 and owned by W. J. D. Pickles, Esq.

CARS OF THE BENTLEY BOYS

This fixed head coupé (since converted to a tourer) by Gurney Nutting on chassis number LR2788 and registered GC 1136 was specially prepared for The Monte Carlo Rally for Cdr. Glen Kidston, of racing fame. Snap filler caps can be seen. Now owned by Waldemar Greyvensteyn, Esq., in South Africa.

Woolf Barnato's special Gurney Nutting coupé complete with cocktail cabinets, with which he beat "The Blue Train" from Monte Carlo to London in 1930 with four hours to spare. Chassis number HM2855, registered GJ 3811, this beautiful car has recently been rebuilt as new by her present owner Hugh Harben, Esq., and was displayed in the Dorchester Hotel in 1968 at the Bentley Drivers Club Annual Dinner and Dance.

BOAT TAILS

The upper version by Barker was their offering for an Olympia Motor Show on a 6½ Litre chassis, and now in the Klein Collection in Pennsylvania.

And the lower edition by Park Ward on a 1929 Speed Six chassis was also exhibited at Olympia, and provides interesting material for comparisons in line.

This fixed head coupé by H. J. Mulliner displays an anti-mud splash feature reminiscent of earlier coaching days.

Both these coupés are felt to be the handiwork of Gurney Nutting. The upper one probably in polished fabric on Weymann principles, favoured in 1929/30 by these coachbuilders as appeasment to chauffeurs, and the lower version equipped with Grebel lamp set, finished in the more common heavier grained fabric fashion.

Royal transportation. The late Duke of Kent's (then Prince George) Speed Six with Freestone and Webb fabric saloon coachwork, and central gear change, which replaced his earlier standard 6½. The registration number YR 11 is thought to have been transferred in turn from His Royal Highness's 1924 Speed Model 3 Litre, and later to be worn by his 8 Litre in 1935.

This close coupled 2-door saloon by Hooper, below, was mounted on chassis number HM2859 and registered GJ 7799, guarantee date from 1st July, 1930.

The American coachbuilders Robert Schuette of New York were responsible for the obvious transatlantic flavour of this saloon, on a Speed Six, whose wheel rims are also in keeping. Photograph taken when owned by that great enthusiast Carl Mueller, Esq.

Messrs. Vanden Plas (1923) England Ltd., used the description of "Flexible Saloon" for this body on a standard 6½, and added a continental touch with the Grebel lamps.

Now in the Manx Motor Museum in the Isle of Man, this standard 6½ chassis number TW2713, registered PF 8749, is fitted with coupé coachwork by the Surbiton Carriage Co.

The very unusual and complicated tail treatment should make coachwork identification possible for the knowledgeable, though I prefer to be non-committal over this coupé, whose background of "Holmwood" was one photographer's favourite venue at that time.

This striking coupé by Gurney Nutting belonging to Dr. J. Blunt in Australia is mounted on chassis number FR2640 whose guarantee dated from 27th July, 1929.

The large rear travelling trunk fitted to this Vanden Plas tourer, registered YT 1929 on chassis number KD2111, bespeaks of the grand tour. This motor, now owned by Harold Dyer, Esq., obtained its guarantee date on 8th July, 1927.

A slightly cleaner aspect is imparted to this VDP tourer, fitted to a circa 1929 Speed Six by the body sides being brought down hiding the chassis frame from view.

Announcement in The Autocar in 1929 was made to the effect that complete cars, fitted with this Panel Fabric Weymann Saloon body, were now obtainable from the manufacturers, who previously had only supplied the chassis.

Neither of these two saloons has been definitely identified, though it is interesting to note how much more modern the lower car appears with its extended doors over the chassis.

Variations on the two seater coupé theme. The upper drop head with dicky seat by Gurney Nutting presents the familiar difficulty of storage of the hood cant rails when folded, which problem does not arise in the fixed head version by H. J. Mulliner on chassis number NH2735, registered UV 8639, and owned by W. D. S. Lake, Esq., shown below.

This unusual four light coupé by Lancefield was mounted on chassis number SB2775, registered GH 2027, and supplied by Rootes Ltd. to her first owner, the famous band leader of the 20's and 30's—Ambrose.

Martin Walter produced this fixed head model on chassis SB2761 and registered GJ 755 which now resides in the Klein collection.

And below, the distinctive and complicated trunk gave added character to this Freestone and Webb coach-built sports saloon, registration number YF 499.

The beautifully clean lines of this owner driver saloon by Park Ward on chassis number FR2628, registered GF 6692, impart an air of ageless dignity.

Though the fabric finish of this H. J. Mulliner saloon and general lines suggest an aura of the 20's, this motor, registered KG 2472, chassis No. SB2751, didn't receive her guarantee until 1931, owner William Nicholson, Esq.

Mystery page! Often photographs were unearthed with no information attached, and these three are all unidentified but H. J. Mulliner is a fair guess for the top one.

With the absence of any definite gen, Freestone and Webb is considered the most likely firm responsible for the middle motor, and the rather sportif sedanca de ville possibly emanated from Gurney Nutting.

These two pages show four interpretations of one theme, that of the rugged touring car in the best Dornford Yates style. Above on chassis number FR2646, registered GK 2466 with strong V.D.P. leanings, the result of D. L. P. Humfrey's own hard work.

And below, Philip Blake's superb rebuild by Hofmann and Burton with coachwork supervised by Basil Mountford, Esq., from a hotch-potch of 6½ Litre parts employing chassis number LB2330 and registered UL 34 which graced The Dorchester Hotel in 1967, daringly finished in white with maroon mudguards.

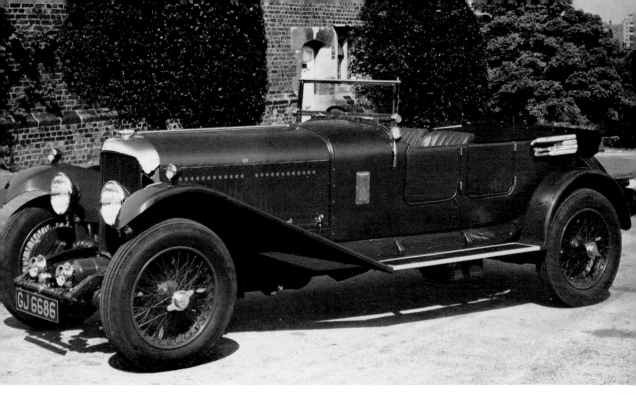

Possibly one of the finest and most meticulous reconstructions undertaken and so generously described in the B.D.C. Review by her creator Brian Morgan, Esq. A Vanden Plas replica on chassis number LR2782, registered GJ 6686, now owned by R. E. Bill, Esq.

H. M. Bentley and Partners' touch (if a little Mercedes-like) is very apparent in this lowered version (circa 1935) with traditional louvred valences hiding the chassis frame of J. Coates' 1927 11ft. wheelbase Speed Six conversion registered BXB 8.

The "Le Mans" touch is obvious in both these specials. In the upper case Guy Shoosmith believes in protecting his 45 gallon petrol tank by placing it within the frame of chassis number HM2865, which originally bore a Gurney Nutting sports saloon, registered GK 8450.

Douglas Symonds, however, threw caution to the winds with authentic Speed Six "Le Mans" tank exposed and vulnerable at the rear of chassis number KR2697, shortened to a wheelbase of 10ft. 10in. to fit his then current garage. A Kensington Gardens Champion in 1963, and registered GH 723, now the property of B. M. Lee, Esq.

This specially constructed Thrupp and Maberly boat tailed body was executed for an Indian Maharajah's big game hunting expeditions.
The rear spotlight could be detached and a long cable wound from the drum mounted on the running board which enabled night sorties to be indulged in. The wood-grained paintwork was a popular feature of the period.

UV 8556 (now in the happy possession of P. R. W. Jupe, Esq., seen here), returned from residence in North Borneo, where she made fastest vintage sports car time in the hands of H. A. Stonor, Esq., at the Sinpag Pulai Hill Climb and equalled the best Jaguar time in May 1955.

This fixed head coupé by H. J. Mulliner, last registered in U.K. as BPO 468 on chassis number LB2348, is now in the possession of Henry Austin Clarke, Jnr., and on view in his extensive automobile collection at Long Island in U.S.A.

Below. Keep the hood line low was undoubtedly Hooper's idea in this tourer, now owned by Alan Wood, Esq., in Toronto, when low screens were the fashion, and traffic did not have its current congestion necessitating the utmost visibility.

Re-registered as RLE 21, probably to take advantage of the post-war £10 taxation system, this tourer by Barker on chassis number FA2513 belonging to H. J, K. Townshend, Esq., employs scuttle cowls of a shape peculiar to this coachbuilder, and below the Speed Six with registration number GU 2801 was rebodied by Windovers in the late 30's with this chamfered edge touring coachwork, incorporating unusual running board treatment.

Two specially built new saloons of around 1936. The upper one by Brigden of Brighton replaced a Gurney Nutting saloon on a 12ft. 8½in. wheelbase chassis DH2212, first guaranteed on 21st June, 1927, and registered YH 9207, owner George Strathdee, Esq.

This lower version was created by Corsica and finished in deep olive green with bold chromium moulding, and was offered for £575 by Sessions in 1937.

The Sammy Davis-Clive Dunfee "Le Mans" Speed Six of 1930, chassis number HM2869, registered GF 8511 as converted by Sagito, a pen name for S. Thomas, Esq. The present owner P. M. Price, Esq., has now returned this historic car to near original state.

The Australian constabulary ordered two Speed Sixes in 1930 for their special Police Patrol, fitted with identical large saloon coachwork of local origin, chassis numbers LR2783 and LR2785.
Below. Sagito's handiwork seen again, here on an early 6½, with the usual radiator shutters added.

Whereas Vanden Plas produced most of the open bodies fitted to vintage Bentleys, Messrs. J. Gurney Nutting, who were later absorbed in the Jack Barclay empire, made the majority of the saloon and coupé coachwork, and on these two pages we can see three of their Olympia Motor Show stands.

In the upper left, an early standard 6½, before the dynamo was moved to beneath the radiator (probably 1927), fitted with an enclosed drive limousine body, incorporating unusual steel windscreen pillars.

Below this is a neat fabric close coupled sports saloon with division and fitted companion sets in the partition, thought to have been shown in 1928.

Above is another standard 6½ of similar design, which appeared at the 1929 Show, with that glamorous fixed head Speed Six coupé, as depicted on page 53, whose elegant contours can be seen above the bonnet—and beyond a variety of different body styling such as we shall never see again.

The accent on Motoring and its great achievements has often been the main theme of the Lord Mayor's Show and here in 1929 what more appropriate machine than this Speed Six chassis, still with its test rig body attached, towing Sir Malcolm Campbell's "Bluebird", world land speed record holder, here in Napier Lion engined form, a connection so nearly to be more firmly established some 18 months later, with the proposed merger of these two famous British concerns.

CHAPTER THREE

$4\frac{1}{2}$ LITRE

Development of the Big Six began 2 years before the advent of the 4 cylinder $4\frac{1}{2}$ Litre engine, which had its debut in the 1927 Le Mans race, to become the first Bentley victim in the famous "White House" pile up. Before this misadventure, Frank Clement had clearly shown the enormous potential of the new engine, breaking the lap record time and time again, and even now 42 years later this 4398 c.c. engine still provides the most popular and most reliable means of having fun in club races.

By 1925 the 3 Litre engine had been extended for competitive purposes about as far as it was safe to take it. Greater power and speed were required if Bentley supremacy was to be maintained with larger cars contending, so a more powerful unit was envisaged. This, W.O. provided very ably in an enlarged version of the 3 Litre car of basically the same specification. Eight years of strenuous use of this design had proved its reliability, and if critics now murmur "cross-shaft gears" — these components had rarely ever to be replaced before World War II, when many 3 and $4\frac{1}{2}$ Litre cars had topped 200,000 miles.

During its production life from 1927 until the closing of the old company in 1931 few modifications were deemed necessary, perhaps the greatest being the introduction of the plate type clutch in 1929, replacing the earlier cone variety. The very late cars produced in 1930 had the heavy blower crankshaft fitted as standard practice, providing practically unburstable and extremely smooth power.

In standard Vanden Plas tourer form the maximum speed was about 92 m.p.h. though "Le Mans" replicas, which could be obtained by the public employing the higher 3.3 to 1 back axle ratio, could top the hundred mark and subsequent tuning has increased this velocity to around 120 in a few special versions.

Brief Specification: 100 mm. bore $\times$ 140 mm. stroke, 4398 c.c.
                             4 cylinder single overhead camshaft engine.
                             Wheelbase: 9ft. $9\frac{1}{2}$in. and 10ft. 10in.
                             Track: 4ft. 8in.

Number of cars made: 662. Plus 6 R.C. series produced from spares by the new company.

The first 4½ Litre, chassis number ST3001, registered YH 3196, and first Bentley to become involved in that epic "White House" pile up of 1927, showing the close resemblance to the then current 3 Litre model. During her debut, before the crash, she again and again broke the lap record in the hands of F. C. Clement, and the following year with Bamuto and Rubin won this classic event.

Below, the registration number YU 3250 is very familiar, but not everyone has seen Bernard Rubin's personal 1928 "Le Mans" replica in her original form before being returned to the works for experimental super-charging exercises, and later to become one of the four Birkin/Paget team cars.
It will be noted that fold flat windscreens seldom were featured in those days on touring Bentleys. Chassis number HF3187, engine HF3192, first guaranteed 17th February, 1928, later to become chassis HB3404/R (R for Rubin) with third Blower engine SM3903.

A "one off" two seater by Vanden Plas. Flaps were later added to those abbreviated mudguards to provide some small degree of weather protection.

Seen below are J. H. Hanley and R. H. Dutton, two Oxford undergraduates (presenting a neater appearance than some students today), with their special 1929 4½ Litre tourer, with several "Le Mans" modifications, which they took to the United States to attack the Coast to Coast record for the 3,200 miles, then standing at 77 hrs. 40 minutes. The registration number was UV 6088.

Drop head coupés all. The top one, by Hooper, was executed to a private owner's special specification. Its boa constrictor horn will be seen behind the spare wheel.

As far as is known, only two of this model were made by Victor Broom of Camden Town, while the car below is a mystery motor, but thought to be by Maythorn's craftsmen.

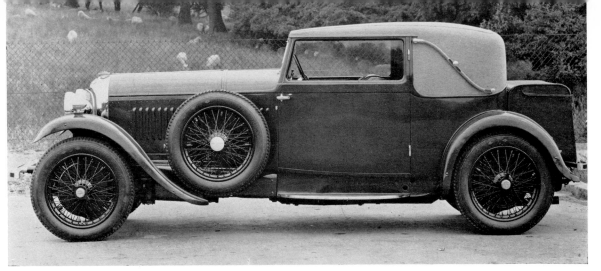

Complete defeat is conceded as to the identity of this extremely neat fixed head coupé.

The central all fabric body, however, is known to be by Maythorn, on chassis number HB3417, first guaranteed on 12th July, 1929 and registered UV 3810, while the bottom car is by Gurney Nutting, employing the smooth polished fabric finish, which was a compromise for chauffeurs who disliked the coarse grained variety of material.

This conservative fabric saloon was specially constructed by Hoopers for Mr. Oppenheimer and supplied in September 1928.

Though the upper of these two fabric saloons is known to be by Vanden Plas on chassis number MR3377, registered KW 5856 and guaranteed 20th April, 1929, the car below is unidentified, though there are some definite Gurney Nutting features evident.

Both these saloons emanate from Gurney Nutting, the upper car being the one built for H.R.H. The Prince of Wales (later Edward the Eighth) with special golf club lockers, raised window sills, interior operated spot lamps, and semaphore indicators, registered UV 6, while the more orthodox version below was their standard offering costing £1,495 in 1929.

The only known boat tailed example by Jarvis on a 4½, chassis number NT3145, and registered PH 6093, here seen as delivered when new, since when a one piece front screen and twin smaller aero screens on the split rear decking have been substituted for the more period original V styling shown. The present owner is Robin Hames, Esq.

The rear seat passengers of Geoffrey Sandwith's 1927 V.D.P. tourer have the luxury of an Auster screen to protect them, on chassis number ST3015, registered MP 974, this model having the deeper doors and metal panelled coachwork.

Another more touring version, this time by Harrison on chassis number PL3494, and originally registered KX 2934, owned by K. S. H. Walker, Esq.

Two pages of drop heads. The upper one is by Salmons, fitted in about 1936 to chassis number RL3429, registered XV 9363 owned by W. J. Chapman, Esq.

Though well known in earlier life to W. O. Bentley's housekeeper, the coachbuilder's name cannot be given with authority, for this all weather body, registration number GF 6250.

Gurney Nutting's special Olympia Show car for 1930, with disappearing hood and float type running boards on chassis number PB3542 and registered GC 4073, was finished in deep green. Guarantee date 15th March, 1930.

Surprisingly enough this special body by Charlesworth affords accommodation for 2, 4 or 6 persons, and is said to have been designed with a view to baffling the L.M.S. Railway over appropriate charges for their toll bridges. Mounted on chassis number AD3658 and registered SB 3535, she is owned by Dr. J. Jamieson.

Specially made for long distance touring by Gurney Nutting, this grey fabric all weather motor was the pride of Mrs. Jewell's eye, and is believed to be still in the family's possession.

Familiar to Kensington Gardens habituées, Douglas Symonds' beautifully restored Salmons all weather saloon on chassis number AB3351, registered GU 404 and now owned by S. Creamer, Esq.

When last seen by the writer in 1960, this Gurney Nutting fabric saloon still had most of the original works seals intact, and full documentary evidence to substantiate the history of one ownership since new. Chassis number FS3168 and registered KR 5928.

A neat saloon by Vanden Plas and a one-time Kensington Gardens Class winner, very smart in its Royal Blue finish, with Dove Grey fabric top.

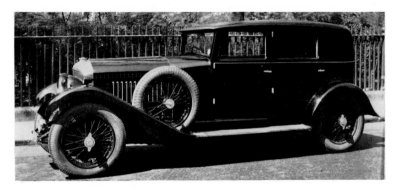

Above, an H. J. Mulliner fabric saloon built on Weymann principles and below, another fabric saloon this time by Martin Walter on chassis number UK3289.

Discs were rare on the open sports models, the only 4½ I knew of being J. C. Sword's, still retained by the family after his collection had been auctioned in Scotland. The Vanden Plas car shown here is as delivered when new.

A Gurney Nutting tourer with central body beam, when owned by Lord Bury, registration number UL 6400, but where is she now?

This Gill bodied drop head is thought to be a "one off", here seen at a joint Rolls-Royce and Bentley Blenheim meeting, she recently came into the market offered by D. Margulies, Esq.

Also probably unique is this Windovers coupé on chassis number XL3114, registered O X 8415.

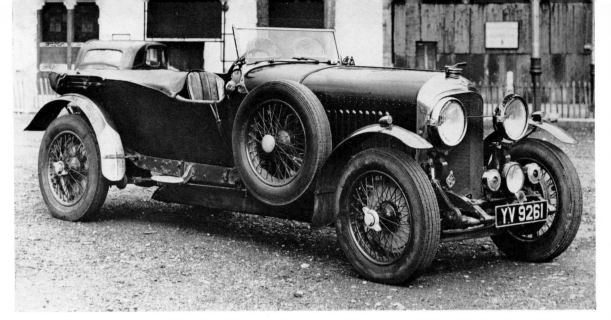

Registered YV 9261, a "T.T." replica, for several years owned by my good friend Stanley Sedgwick, which enlivened early post-war Continental tours and provided the author with practically non-stop motoring to the Belgian Spa Grand Prix in typical Sedgwick fashion. now in the possession of D. G. Braxton, Esq., chassis number MF3174.

For the 1928 "Le Mans" race, the Bentley team comprised three 4½ Litres, of which two were equipped with this special Vanden Plas bodywork, with rounded tail and semi-recessed spare wheel and the higher mounted petrol tank. F. C. Clement is seen here in No. 2. The sister car No. 3, driven by Birkin and Chassagne, subsequently had its body damaged by fire and this was replaced by the more traditional style of coachwork incorporating the tool locker between body and special 25 gallon tank. No. 2, chassis number KM3088, was registered YW 2557, bought from the company in 1930 by Laughlin Rose, Esq., still owned by his son, T. D. L. Rose, Esq.

The third production 4½, chassis number ST3003, was one of the eight 9ft. 9½in. wheelbase versions made, and this one, registered YT 7756 (25th August, 1927) has convertible coachwork by Mulliners.

Above, a 1929 model, registered UV 8226, fitted with this fixed head fabric coupé by H. J. Mulliner and below we have a late (19th September, 1931) heavy crankshaft edition on chassis XT3626 fitted with a Mayfair coupé and registered KX 7520.

What will they think of next? The film men's efforts to create a vehicle suitable for Terry-Thomas in "School for Scoundrels". First time to my knowledge that a 4 cylinder Bentley had its exhaust manifold on the off side!

The Corsica coachworks produced several new touring bodies in the '30's as replacements for less sporting originals, and this one on chassis number NX3461 (1st August, 1929), registered UV 6341, is a typical example, owned by M. B. Gaudin, Esq.

Quite an improvement on the form shown on the opposite page, and looking like the genuine article, is this "Le Mans" replica created by Hofmann and Burton for Bentley collector, Charles Noble, Esq., of New York. YX 550, chassis number PM3272 is here seen gracing the Dorchester Hotel Ballroom.

Another H. M. Bentley and Partners conversion, this time retaining four seats, and "Le Mans" tank at the rear, on chassis number PM3262 which, originally registered as EW 5578, bore a Maddox saloon, now owned by D. E. Phipps, Esq., in South Africa.

Another short chassis 9ft. 9½in. wheelbase model now in South Africa and fitted with a Harrison touring body on chassis number TN1555. One would have thought, as distributors, the company should know how to spell Bentley! Below a Cadogan tourer on chassis number PL3487.

One of the six special RC series chassis built up from spares by the new company in about 1936, and this one, chassis number RC45 and registered GME 152, is fitted with Vanden Plas coachwork and owned by V. M. Wingate, Esq.

While below is yet another of the 8 "Shorties" with V.D.P. coachbuilt body, registered WT 43 and owned by W. Thompson, Esq.

Since the war a few specialist body builders have produced replicas of the Vanden Plas tourers. These are often indistinguishable from the genuine article, and none are more authentic than those by Phillips as shown here, mounted on the seventh $4\frac{1}{2}$ Litre, chassis number ST3007, registered in June, 1927, as YU 7455. Possibly the only criticisms the purist might offer are that the windscreen would not have been in folding down form, but of the three panel pattern typical of that period, and the Lucas P100 headlamps are from a slightly later car.

This B.D.C. Kensington Gardens champion of 1966 is owned by R. W. Colton, Esq.

CHAPTER FOUR

SUPERCHARGED
$4\frac{1}{2}$ LITRE

The Blower Bentleys as they were generally known, were undoubtedly the most controversial, as well as the most exciting and glamorous of all Bentleys made.

Early in 1929 Bernard Rubin's 1928 "Le Mans" replica $4\frac{1}{2}$ was returned to the works for experimenting with an Amherst Villiers supercharger fitted between the front dumbirons ahead of the radiator. This modification was made at Birkin's request, in search of greater speed from the $4\frac{1}{2}$, with a view to victory at Le Mans.

W.O., however, believed that an equal increase in speed and a much greater degree of reliability were obtainable from the Speed Six machine. Subsequent results in competition proved him correct.

It must have brought some relief when this motor departed to the Birkin and Couper Stable at Welwyn to become No. 3 car of the Birkin/Paget team of supercharged cars, her registration number, a 1928 one (YU 3250), is well known to every Bentley enthusiast and collector of Lesney model cars.

However, to be accepted by the authorities, The Automobile Club de l'Ouest, for Le Mans, a batch of 50 production cars were constructed, and W.O. is known to have attributed to this a large proportion of the blame for the financial failure of the old company.

The appeal of these cars is reflected now, with a higher percentage of this model than any other Bentley still in existence, as it was in the days of the Bentley boys of 1929/31, its every aspect denoted a car only suitable for "he-men", and with this brute force appearance went a performance to support it.

Brief Specification: 100 mm. bore $\times$ 140 mm. stroke, 4398 c.c.
4 cylinder single overhead camshaft engine.
Wheelbase: 10ft. 10in.
Track: 4ft. 8in.

Number of cars made including two 9ft. $9\frac{1}{2}$in. special Birkin cars: 55.

"THE BROOKLANDS BATTLESHIP"

Here Tim Birkin's famous outer circuit single seater Blower 4½ is shown in four of her various guises. With racing number 5 Sir Henry is seen at her first showing at the B.A.R.C. 6 Hour Race, on 29th June, 1929, at Brooklands, fitted with the special VDP 4 seater body, with which she was to compete in the TT in August, and the Irish Grand Prix of that year, with her sister car driven by Bernard Rubin.

The lower picture illustrates the shape taken during the winter of 1929/30, when all three Birkin/Paget team cars were entirely rebuilt, with a fourth added to their number, and in which form she is best known to all pre-war Bentley fans. Chassis number HB3402, with the first supercharged engine, number ST3901 and registered UU 5871.

Acquired by the late Peter Robertson-Roger, Esq., in 1939 as a source of engine replacement for his 1930 Birkin Pau car, blown up at Donington Park. She was rebuilt into a two seater (almost) version of her track form, and later purchased from John Morley, Esq., by Rusty Russ-Turner to be added to his collection of various models of supercharged Bentleys.

Caffyns remodelled the original 1930 cowl and her old Brooklands radiator replaced the previously exposed and lowered Bentley shaped one, and doubtless if Rusty hadn't been of such ample proportions (the wind is helping a little), the original single seater body, which he still preserves, would also have been mounted, into which Birkin, of small stature, fitted comfortably.

The lower picture illustrates "The Brooklands Battleship" as she is today.

Of the 50 production Blower cars, 26 were fitted with Vanden Plas open bodies and in most cases the later editions took shape in two door form. This flared mudguarded model is identical to that in the Briggs Cunningham collection.

By late 1930, Vanden Plas had moved with the times in producing the beautiful clean lines as depicted here on chassis number SM3924, registered GO 2641 (guarantee date 10th April, 1931) and now in The Harrah Automobile Collection in Reno. Those front mudguards incorporate tool lockers.

This two seater coupé by Gurney Nutting fitted to chassis number MS3928, registered FG 6667, was the third Blower car with the ribbed supercharger casing, and the first with the reinforced crankcase, now with Charles Noble's other 4 Blower Bentleys in New York.

One of the six only saloons fitted to the Supercharged 4½, this one by Freestone and Webb, was finished in two shades of grey and priced at £1,695. It will be noted flush fitting sunshine roofs had now arrived.

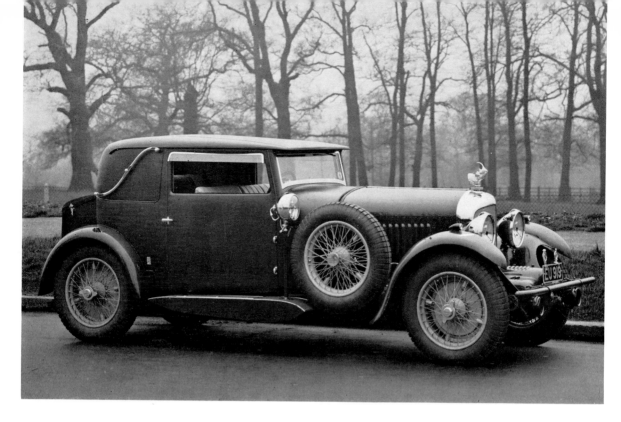

Above, EU 919 as she was originally, with her fixed head coupé coachwork by Maythorn, later converted to drop head form and afterwards fitted with an unusual open body, before her monumental rebuild by Tony Townshend (see opposite page). Below, the last batch of six Blower cars, this one being chassis number M3946 and registered GY 3905, were all acquired by Jack Barclay and fitted with drop head coupé bodies by Vanden Plas. Present owner W. J. Hindson, Esq.

EU 919 as she is today in the Klein collection in Pennsylvania, and here seen at Oulton Park when participating in "The Bentley Snowball Run". Tony Townshend's "Le Mans" treatment complete with 50 gallon rear tank to chassis number SM3905, being admired at her first presentation.

And below, the genuine article. Birkin's 1930 Le Mans No. 9 mount, chassis number HB3403, engine SM3902, registration number UU 5872, here wearing No. 8's number plates which she used for about 37 years (now both cars have their correct registration plates), as rebuilt by H. J. K. Townshend, Esq., for Stanley Sears, Esq. No. 8 has also now been rejuvenated for Neil Corner, Esq.

Above, registered UR 9155, chassis number HR3977 which was a special Birkin chassis series number, with the 2 seater body fitted earlier to Tim's Outer Circuit motor, and apparently wearing the slanted louvred bonnet top from the same car. This "Bolide" earned fame in the hands of the late Alick Pitts, Esq., with a fastest sports car time at Brighton, and is now owned by R. Melville-Smith, Esq. Below, chassis number MS3949, originally one of the last six fitted with Vanden Plas coupé coachwork, as rebuilt by Competition Cars of Nayland, then re-registered BGH 55, and now in the Scottish collection of E. G. Thomson, Esq.

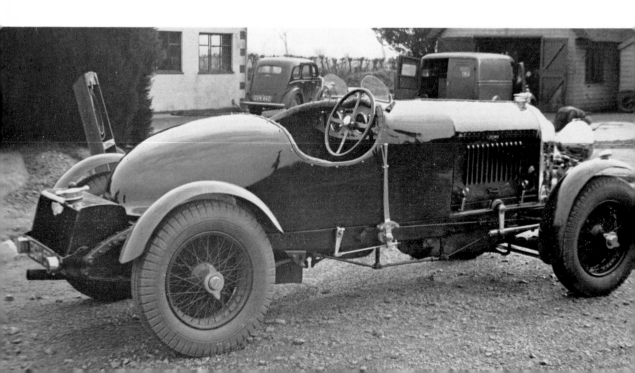

Above, one of the two Blower cars owned by Woolf Barnato, this one with body by Gurney Nutting on chassis number SM3909 and registered GK 6661 (27th November, 1930), has tail treatment reminiscent of the 20/60 Hurlingham Vauxhall of 1930. Below, chassis number MS3944, originally a VDP "Le Mans" replica owned by Scrap Thistlethwayte, Esq., then registered JK 1925 (30th July, 1931), as she is now after being rebuilt by Mr. Johnson in Canada, further rejuvenated by Cameron Peck, Esq., and now living in California.

It is said the camera cannot lie, but even allowing for an extended bonnet, it is believed that the steering column must also have been extended. Perhaps R. J. Whitaker, Esq., one time owner and great "Blower" supporter, can enlighten us. The original coachwork was by Vanden Plas on chassis number MS3930 and registered YY 3692.

Below, a motor familiar to all "BDC" members, and Lesney "Matchbox" series collectors, the long chassis (10ft. 10in. wheelbase) Birkin-Paget team car, the first experimental supercharged 4½ installed in Bernard Rubin's 1928 "Le Mans" replica, chassis number HF3187 (later to become chassis number HB3404/R) and registered YU 3250. Present owner Harry Rose, Esq.

CHAPTER FIVE

8 LITRE

The greatest of them all is the author's own personal opinion and, if feats of performance were needed to uphold this statement, two cars alone would give worthy support to this—the immortal motor evolved by L. C. McKenzie "Mac", for the late Forrest Lycett, whose creation still ably acquits itself in the present ownership of Stanley Sears, and the one time Brooklands outer circuit record holder, the Barnato Hassan with a lap of 143.11 m.p.h. to its credit and still being hurled to victory in Historic Racing Car events by Keith Schellenberg.

It is remarkable that after the passage of 38 years, out of the total production of 100 cars, both in 12ft. and 13ft. wheelbase lengths, approximately sixty remain and after some diligent research, the writer has been able to unearth some history on 97 of these superb machines.

The 8 Litre was basically an enlarged edition of the Speed Six (probably W.O.'s favourite creation), but employing a new lower chassis frame, with out-set rear springs and an 'F' series gear box differing from all previous Bentley design in having its casing split down the centre, as opposed to the square box with a lid on top, as previously used in all earlier cars. This layout allowed for larger bearings providing additional strength, and quietness in operation.

In absolutely standard form as sold towards the end of 1930 (the first models appeared at the October Olympia Motor Show) this magnificent machine would top a genuine 100 m.p.h. bearing limousine coachwork and eight persons sitting inside.

It is felt that the advent of this remarkably silent machine may well have influenced the Rolls-Royce company to make their bid for the assets of the old Bentley company, as it was known that an advanced 6 Litre edition was on the drawing board at Napiers, where W.O. was already engaged on his new brain child, the Bentley/Napier that never was.

Brief Specification: 110 mm. bore × 140 mm. stroke, 7982.81 c.c.
6 cylinder, coupling rod driven, single o/h camshaft engine.
Wheelbases: 12ft. and 13ft.
Track: 4ft. 8in.

Number of cars made: 100

Naked and justifiably unashamed, the massive chassis of the 8 Litre, and, below, the highly polished engine of the "Le Mans" like fabric sports 4 seater, so effectively created by Tony Townshend, and providing a full house in Reg Parker's vintage Bentley stable, chassis number YR5077.

There was difficulty in choosing the correct chapter for this one, the first experimental 8 Litre, as developed by W.O., using an early 6½ Litre frame with bored out cylinder block, still in reversed position to all other 8 Litres. She originally wore a very square fabric saloon body known as "The Box" which was replaced by H. M. Bentley and Partners with the existing VDP coachwork, now in the possession of R. D. Weary, Jnr., in the States.

Another 8 Litre to find her way across the Atlantic, chassis number YR5086, and first fitted with a Thrupp and Maberly limousine body, this dual cowl tourer is now owned by Scott Appleby, Esq.

Cars of the nobility. The Bustard family's 8 Litres, both finished in black with fine white lining. R. L. Bustard's 12ft. wheelbase chassis number YF5025 and registered IA 9500, had four light coachwork by

Freestone and Webb, while A. U. Bustard's limousine body by Thrupp and Maberly was mounted on the 13ft. wheelbase chassis of number YF5086, their respective prices when new being £2,680 and £3,055.

Above, another Bentley from the fabulous Harrah collection of over 1300 cars in Reno, a Windovers Drop Head Coupé, for many years owned by Briggs Cunningham. The twin steps are not an affectation, as I've proved it to be possible to enter the rear compartment without disturbing the front seat passengers. Chassis number YR5080.

Below, this Lancefield body on chassis number YM5044 and registered GX 6152 with disappearing hood, while equipped with rear deck and screen, had no provision for side curtains, a true tourer.

As she was when the property of that famous racing driver of the 30's Witney Straight, Esq., and then fitted with a preselector gear box. Chassis number YF5023, registered GP 31, with sedanca coupé by Gurney Nutting, was later dismantled to provide a basis for a McKenzie 4/8 special tourer for R. W. D. Carr, Esq

Below, a fixed head coupé by Freestone and Webb mounted on chassis number YR5081.

Two of L. C. McKenzie, Esq.'s ("*Mac*" *the High Priest of Bentleys*) *lowered 8 Litre specials, both with coachwork by Corsica. The upper version has been remodelled by F. L. M. Panelcraft Ltd. for Briggs Cunningham, and is mounted on chassis YX5117, registered GY 88, while below chassis number YM5050 and registered UL 7 is seen with her owner for so many years, the late Oliver Goodwin, who acquired this car as a memorial to his son killed in action in the R.A.F.—one of "the few"—and now taken over by Mrs. Goodwin.*

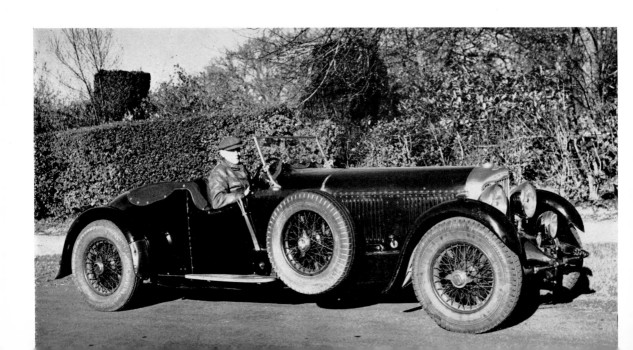

GP 1999, chassis number YF5005, with the Thrupp and Maberly drop head coupé body with disappearing
hood as displayed at the 1930 Motor Show.
When I saw her in 1940 at Windsor the coachwork had deteriorated, doubtless contributing to the decision
of Jack Broadhead to rebuild her in the guise seen below, here a Concours d'Elegance winner at Blenheim
in 1966 and now owned by G. W. Rothwell, Esq.

A replacement sedanca de ville for Mrs. Nea V. Flemmick, accounting for the more modern lines than the original body, on chassis number YM5050. The car was later cannibalised by McKenzie to provide material for A. C. Clark's special and re-registered as UL7, and now owned by Stanley Sedgwick Esq.

Below, Guy Shoosmith's H. J. Mulliner 4 light limousine on chassis YM5038, registered GW 2386, a Dorchester Hotel guest in 1967, and wartime mount for the Corps General of Southern Command at Salisbury during the Second World War.

The top car of these four magnificent machines, chassis number YX5115 and registered AG 6917, bears a sports saloon by H. J. Mulliner—premier Bentley at the 1967 Goodwood Pageant and owned by R. Collinson-Cooper, Esq. in Texas.

As she was originally, chassis number YX5117 and registered GY88, fitted with a sports saloon by Gurney Nutting. Now she is in the form as shown on page 116 in the Briggs Cunningham collection.

This impressive saloon with division, on the first production 8 Litre, chassis number YF5001 and registered GK 672, was delivered new to matinee idol of the 20's and 30's Jack Buchanan, and is now in the Klein collection.

This stylish sports saloon fitted to chassis number YM5046 and registered GP 7192, is by the Carlton Carriage Co. This motor has since been dismantled and now forms the basis of Oliver Batten's 4/8 special.

An impressive Kensington Gardens line up. In the foreground, bearing registration number LXA 230, is the last 8 Litre, chassis number YX5125, bought new in 1931 by a Mr. Hewett of Anglesey, who having learned of the probable demise of the old company felt a spare chassis for his special fabric Vanden Plas tourer, fitted to chassis number YX5119 (see page 132) might be a wise precaution. After over 20 years, with the first car still performing impeccably, the necessity for spares was deemed superfluous.
Alec N. Hewett, Esq. (no relation) was lucky enough to acquire this brand new and regularly serviced chassis from its storage, but 100 yards from the birthplace of the first 3 Litre. (Yes, the author used to hopefully pay homage.)

Her new owner had McKenzie lower the line, and tune the engine with treble SU carburettors, before fitting the new three plus two body by Dottridge Bros. of Islington.
Next in line is Briggs Cunningham's modified Corsica tourer, registration number G Y 88, alongside the Lancefield tourer on chassis YM5044 with a Mulliner saloon (registration number G Y 3903 on chassis number YX5110) and the Company's Park Ward demonstration saloon, registration number GP 8271, parked next to what is thought to be Mrs. Eileen Wright's 1928 Weymann Speed Six saloon, well over twelve tons of machinery in six superb machines.

On the opposite page we have some truly potent machinery. The top car of these three special "Bolides" is Frank Sowden's well known competition motor first built up by S. H. Richardson, Esq., employing the engine from chassis number YX5101, and registered PPB 10.

Ever an exciting entry at VSCC and Bentley Silverstone meetings, she has achieved speeds of nearly twice our present legal limit.

The original concept was to retain an occasional four seater body, and the rounded tail was carefully shaped to provide accommodation for the spare wheel behind the rear tonneau.

Lowering an 8 Litre may reduce to some extent the very impressive frontal aspect, but it does at the same time reduce the enormous area for wind resistance imposed by the radiator in its full glory. Forward visibility is also vastly improved and the general handling especially on corners considerably enhanced.

In the centre, now twin turbo supercharged, is John Goddard's McKenzie devised two seater. Somehow Donald, son of the famous "Mac", has squeezed all this power into a strengthened 3 Litre chassis frame to provide what may well be the potentially fastest Bentley in existence.

Some earlier experimentation had been carried out on this car when employing a $6\frac{1}{2}$ Litre unit, in the days when she sported the even more spartan two seater body with rear slab type petrol tank.

John Goddard has more recently had the present bumble tail body made enclosing the rear mounted spare wheel and petrol tank—and once pointed in the right direction her acceleration up the straight at Silverstone is nothing less than shattering.

Kensington Gardens Champion for 1962, at the bottom, is W. A. L. Cook's beautiful pointed tail two seater planned by Bill, and executed for him by Hofmann and Burton in contemporary style, to provide a means of progress the manner of which we shall never see produced again. Chassis number YR5092 and registered GO 4409.

When designing new coachwork on a rebuilt Vintage Bentley, it is essential that the style and spirit of the time be preserved, and in this Bill Cook has succeeded admirably in retaining all the character of the period, yet providing some more modern amenities, the new pattern windscreen wiper and electric fan being two of the more practical modifications. Triple S.U. carburettors are used, and though tuned well beyond standard output, no attempt has been made to transform this into a pure racer, the owner having fast touring only in mind, other potent machinery being maintained for mixing it with the moderns.

The heavy spare wheel lives behind on top of the tapering tail, deeply recessed in a well, from which I must confess I have yet to see it removed by one person unaided, the intention obviously being to ensure its masculine appeal in all respects.

His Royal Highness the Duke of Kent, father of the present Duke, commissioned Thrupp and Maberly in 1935 to produce this special saloon for his 8 Litre chassis, number YR5087. Already the owner of a 3½ Litre Derby built car, he had the registration number YR11 carried forward from his earlier vintage Bentleys. Specially incorporated features were snap filler caps, stoneguards protecting the twin front spot lights, and twin externally mounted fire extinguishers.

And below, the angle from which this motor is seen by most, a three-quarter rear shot of the late Forrest Lycett's immortal motor bought new 12th March, 1931, by McKenzie for Lycett, chassis number YX5121, and then fitted with a Corsica touring body, registration number GW 2926.

"Mac" developed this car to such an extent that in 1959 Lycett was able to record a timed speed of 141 m.p.h. at Herentals in Belgium. Upon Mr. Lycett's death in 1960, it was bequeathed to a worthy charity from which it was later acquired by Stanley Sears.

In very good simple taste, a Gurney Nutting saloon on 13ft. wheelbase, chassis number YM5029, registration number GT 8777, and first guaranteed on 13th January, 1931.

Above, this sedanca de ville by Thrupp and Maberly, finished in blue and black, cost Capt. F. A. Pearson £3039 10s. 0d. in 1931. Below is Park Ward's limousine used for publicity purposes on chassis number YF5022 and registered GN 4110. This seven seater motor now owned by J. W. Alington, Esq., is still almost indistinguishable from new, with original paintwork and upholstery.

Messrs. Vanden Plas produced two sports tourers to the same specification of GP 401 shown above. This one on chassis number YR5095, was supplied to Woolf Barnato, the twin to Mr. Foden, lifelong Bentley enthusiast, on chassis number YX5122. Wing Commander Reggie Presland, the present owner, purchased Barnato's car from him 34 years ago

The beautiful Gurney Nutting tourer seen below was originally supplied to Sir Alexander Kleinwert on chassis number YX5102, registration number PM 9413, but the body has since been removed and fitted to the Major Schreiber 1928 Phantom I Rolls-Royce in which form she exists today.

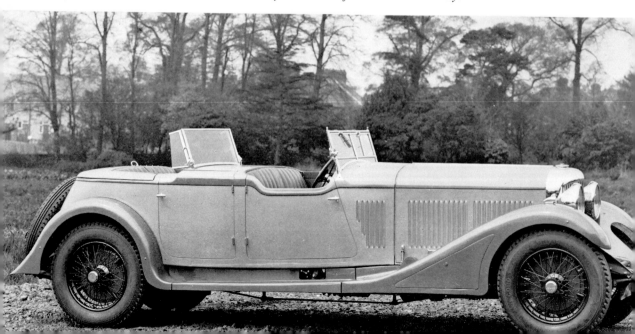

This unusual drop head coupé with disappearing hood was built by Vanden Plas to the special order of Lord Brougham de Vaux, was later removed, and fitted to an Isotta-Fraschini chassis. The 8 Litre chassis number YR5097, and registered GP5, was rebodied with a four seater tourer and is now owned by Dr. Scher in the U.S.A.

Below, Park Ward produced this owner driver saloon, finished in black with green moulding, on 13ft. wheelbase chassis number YM5037, which was the company's demonstrator, and for years a consistent concours winner in the late Stuart Marshall's hands. Registered GP 8271, costing £2,780 when new, she is now owned by William Ruger, Jnr., in the U.S.A.

The top car with all weather body by H. J. Mulliner on chassis number YX5123 and registered GW 1559, was later modified by "Sagito" to present a similar appearance to car No. 4 on this page.

This motor was the second production 8 Litre, chassis number YF5002 and registered GK706, fitted with a lightweight sports saloon by H. J. Mulliner for W. O. Bentley's personal use. She is now owned by Geoffrey Sandwith, Esq.

Owned by his father before the war, this Freestone and Webb coupé on chassis number YF5021 and registered JN 1333, has always been one of the faster 8 Litres, and F. M. Wilcock's speed of 108.2 m.p.h. at Ghent in 1968 will substantiate this.

This "Sagito" modified Mayfair coupé on chassis number YX5124 and registered GX8867, has since been returned to her original state by her present owner, Capt. G. C. Blundell, with long swept front mudguards, and the tool lockers dispensed with.

Another form of tourer by Vanden Plas, differing from that shown on page 126, fitted to chassis number YX5111 and registered CG 1379. She is in the ownership of Major H. W. Whyte.

These two Olympia Motor Show cars of 1930 were both bodied by Gurney Nutting. The upper close coupled saloon was then strikingly finished in biscuit and black on the 12ft. wheelbase chassis number YF5007 and registered GK 7159, the price new was £2,625.

The sedanca de ville below, with front compartment here covered, has often (I think erroneously) been attributed to Kellner of Paris, but this one on chassis number YF5004 and registered GK 8447 was displayed on the Gurney Nutting stand, then finished in dove grey and black, and last seen by the writer before the war drawing up majestically outside the Savoy Hotel. Gurney Nutting's approach to running boards at that time was both varied and distinctive. Now modified considerably for her present owner Lord Cranworth.

Chassis YM5047 originally fitted with a Carlton saloon and registered GY6838, is seen here as the Kensington Gardens champion for 1965, after being rebuilt by Hoffmann and Burton as a sports four seater tourer and finished in British Racing Green. She is now owned by R. M. R. Eckart, Esq.

The car shown below started life as the company's Continental demonstrator with a limousine body on chassis number YF5013 and registered GT 8778. She was rebodied with Hooper all weather coachwork in about 1936, and then later her 13ft. wheelbase was shortened to 11ft. 2in. and the present touring coachwork fitted. Her current owner is Norris Allen, Esq., in the U.S.A.

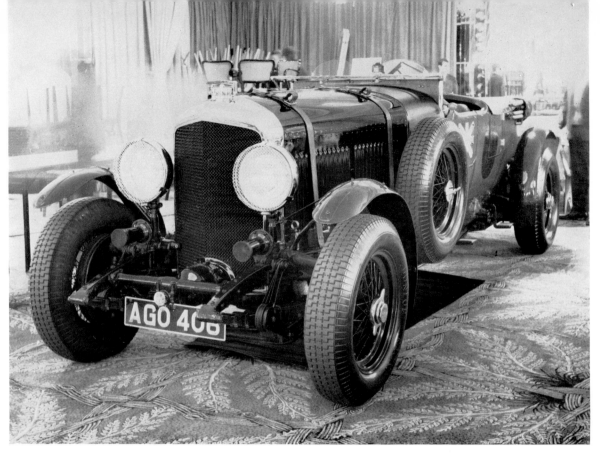

AGO 406 will be remembered at Kensington Gardens, when presented by O. P. Raphael, Esq., with a concours winning shooting brake body. As shown here in The Dorchester Hotel, Tony Townshend's superb rebuild, aided by Phillips' lively interpretation of a "Le Mans" car that never was, is evident. She now lives in Reg Parker's complete "W. O. Bentley" collection. Chassis number YR5077.

Below, Lt. Col. Jacobs wisely retained the original flared mudguards from the Gurney Nutting sports saloon, when rebuilding chassis number YX5112, registration number GP 8441, into a class winning champion at the 1964 Goodwood Pageant.
This dual cowl sports tourer now resides in the U.S.A.

As specially turned out by the old company for her original owner Mr. Hewett, with a very narrow fabric body by Vanden Plas and enormous rear petrol tank dwarfing even the largest "Le Mans" size, chassis number YX5119, registered DM 7853, for which the spare chassis (number YX5125) was purchased in 1931. This car remained until only recently at her first home in Anglesey, and is still entirely unmodified as she left the works in 1931, stoneguards and outside exhausts complete, and now owned by Mr. de Ferranti.

Below, the original owner Sir P. Malcolm Stewart is seen in the Barker boat tail two seater on chassis number YR5099, registration number GN 82, before a subsequent owner modified her to the drop head coupé form she now presents in the ownership of J. McHarg, Esq., who intends to return this car to its original state.

CHAPTER SIX

4 LITRE

This is a sad chapter to write, as this model, hastily introduced in 1931 in a desperate effort on the part of the board of directors to save the company's finances, denoted the impending demise of the old company. They produced a car in that period of depression to match the smaller Rolls-Royce, with a less costly price tag.

It should be emphasised that the engine used in this model had nothing to do with W.O. who could not endorse the decision to employ a power plant of only 3915 c.c. (a 6 cylinder with a Ricardo designed cylinder head employing side exhaust and overhead inlet valves) in the shorter versions of the 8 litre chassis, 11ft. 2in. wheelbase for 39 of the total production of 50 cars, the remaining 11 being 11ft. 8in. wheelbase models.

The engine was obviously unsuited for propelling so much weight, and no time could be given to its development, with the result that this, the last model to emerge from the old Cricklewood works, did nothing for the wonderful Bentley reputation. It was a type of machine foreign to the company's image —an overladen touring motor, whose power to weight ratio could never impart the performance everyone had come to associate as synonymous with the name.

About eleven of this model are still giving their owners pleasure, one in the same family since new.

Jack Barclay acquired a number of these 4 Litre chassis at the very end, and endowed them with coachwork which was probably the most pleasing in line ever seen on any vintage Bentley.

Brief Specification: 85 mm. bore × 140 mm. stroke, 3915 c.c.
6 cylinder side exhaust and overhead inlet valve engine.
Wheelbases: 11ft. 2in. and 11ft. 8in.
Track: 4ft. 8in.
Number of cars made: 50

This is a Gurney Nutting sports
saloon fitted to the 11ft. 2in.
wheelbase chassis of VA4097 and
registered GY 184, with guarantee
date from 10th June, 1931.

The Harrison touring body shown
here is mounted on the long
chassis, number YF4015 and
registered GT 975.
The original owner's preference
for a polished aluminium bonnet
has been retained.

This Mulliner sports saloon on
chassis number VF4008 and
registered GT 8776 was last
heard of in about 1957 when
owned by K. Ralph, Esq.

Another 11ft. 2in. wheelbase, chassis number VA4076, again fitted with a sports saloon by Gurney Nutting with more conservative styling and registered GP 7767, guarantee date from 15th July, 1931.

A special light weight saloon by H. J. Mulliner on chassis number VF4004 and registered GO 8477, which was rescued en route to the breakers yard after the last war and beautifully renovated to her original state in Royal Blue and Black. Her present owner is J. V. Murcott, Esq.

This extremely pretty drop head coupé body by Vanden Plas is fitted to chassis number VA4083, registration number GP 8573, and was reconditioned to as-new order by N. W. McCaw in 1948, but has since disappeared.

Freestone and Webb were responsible for the sports saloon below on chassis number VA4084, registration number GX 1701. Only perhaps the old style sunshine roof gives evidence of her guarantee date of 23rd April, 1931.

CHAPTER SEVEN

VINTAGE BENTLEY
IN ACTION

Though this chapter dwells largely upon the racing aspect of the marque over the years, it must be borne in mind that at all times the Bentley was foremost a touring car. Their appearance in competition between 1920 and 1930 was for publicity purposes, and from the experience gained in these exercises the strain in their thoroughbred pedigree gained additional strength. Their reliability, now extensively proven over fifty years, was then backed by a five year guarantee.

One could devote a lifetime to the delightful pursuit of writing about Bentleys in competition throughout the years. It would be a never ending work, for as this is being written, the London to Sydney Marathon includes one private entry to stimulate the imagination of any amateur motoring enthusiast, that of the 38 year old 8 Litre Bentley of Keith Schellenberg, pitted against the giants of the modern day industry.

So the next 23 pages can only give the briefest glimpse of their endeavours, and one hopes that one day these may be chronicled in a manner fit to do justice to their record; for, when one considers that the total production of the old company amounted to only 3031 cars all told, to be able to muster 50 years later a known third of that lineage still capable of maintaining their original performances is a feat I venture to state we shall never see repeated.

The first Bentley team, and a victorious one, the three Tourist Trophy race cars of 1922. No. 9 was driven by W. O. Bentley, chassis number 72, whose correct registration number was ME 3115, finishing 4th at 52.69 m.p.h. In the centre, W.O. is seated in Car No. 6 which Hawkes drove into 5th place, this was chassis number 74, registered ME 3494. And finally on the right is Clement with Car No. 3, in which he finished 2nd at 55.21 m.p.h., chassis number 42 and registered ME 1884. These three cars were awarded the team prize and apart from the 1922 Indianapolis motor, were the only Bentleys fitted with this form of flat radiator.

It is recorded that the cost of the preparation for all three cars amounted to only £75 for the very few modifications found necessary from standard form, an extremely modest outlay and rather different from present-day expenditure in developing a team of modern racing cars.

Frank Clement at Brooklands about to set out in search of new records with his T.T. car. He was the company's first official works driver, and a competitor in every Le Mans race entered by Bentleys. Below, Woolf Barnato with the first 4½ Litre, before the Essex Club's 6-Hour Race in 1928 at Brooklands.

The Birkin Paget team for Le Mans 1930. No. 7 was to have been driven by Bevis Harcourt-Wood and Jack Dunfee, but due to insufficient time, the compression plates could not be removed from all three cars, this last moment change was made so that pure benzol could be used in place of the low octane petrol available. So chassis number HB3404/R, registration number YU 3250 was a non-starter.

With racing number 8, the new fourth car of Paget stable, chassis number HR3976 and registered UR 6571, driven by Ramponi and Dr. Benjafield, who took the lion's share of the wheel, due to Ramponi's illness during the night hours, she completed 144 laps and was lying in 3rd place when a piston collapsed after nearly 21 hours running.

No. 9, Chassagne at the wheel with Tim Birkin beside him, after weighing in, clearly displaying those extra telltale bolts in her chassis, evidence of the repairs necessitated by her cracked frame sustained during the 1930 Double Twelve Race at Brooklands. No. 9 completed 138 laps before retiring, but during her epic tyre destroying run she took the lap record at 89.69 m.p.h., to stand for all time for the course as it was then.

Old Number One Speed Six, with the men who drove her to victory at Le Mans in 1929, Sir Henry Birkin, Bart., and Woolf Barnato. Barnato also drove the same car to victory again in 1930 on the Sarthe circuit, that year partnered by Glen Kidston. Her registration number was MT 3464, and she has since been dismantled and various parts found their way into two special 8 Litres.

Below, the car which finished second at Le Mans in 1930 (then driven by Clement and Watney), here seen at Brooklands with Woolf Barnato and Frank Clement before setting out to win the 1930 Double Twelve Race, number 2 for this event, chassis number HM2868, registered GF 8507, now owned by Carl Mueller. The model Bentley is thought to be conducted by Master Carew, Junior.

Yes! we have seen the picture before but it makes such splendid viewing, I had to include it.
The start of Junior Car Clubs Double Twelve Hour Race at Brooklands, 9/10th May, 1930, with six Bentleys
entered. No 2 (6½ Litre) F. C. Clement and Woolf Barnato, 1st at Brooklands, 1st at 86.68 m.p.h.; No. 3 (6½ Litre) S. C. H. Davis
and Clive Dunfee, 2nd at 85.68 m.p.h.; No. 10 (4½ Litre) M. O. de B. Durand and T. K. Williams (retired);
No. 6 (4½ S) J. D. Benjafield and Baron D'Erlanger (retired); No. 4 (4½ S) Sir Henry Birkin and Jean
Chassagne (retired with cracked chassis frame); and No. 5 (4½ S) has already accelerated out of the picture
under the paddock bridge, driven by Glen Kidston and Jack Dunfee (retired).

W. B. Scott with his "Le Mans" model 3 Litre at Brooklands for the Essex Car Club's Six Hour Race at Brooklands 12th May, 1928, chassis number ML 1501, registered YF 2503 (now owned by Norris Kennard, Esq.). A sister car, chassis number ML1513 and registered YV 8588, was driven by Humphrey Cook, and last seen by the author at the Mena House Hotel, Cairo, in 1942.
Below, the Birkin team of 1929 en route for the Tourist Trophy Race in Ireland, stopping at The Hand Hotel, Llangollen. Sir Henry Birkin's Speed Six (UL 4203) on the left. Rubin's race car (UU 5872) Bernard behind the radiator. Birkin's car (UU 5871) with Tim in front, and still wearing her 1928 "Le Mans" blade type mudguards (YU 3250) the first experimental blower car.

"Men at Work." If Birkin and Couper's stable had a publicity agent, he was doing his stuff that day, depicting activity on one of the two short chassis Blower cars.

The Barnato Hassan, one time Brooklands Outer Circuit record holder with a lap of 143.1 m.p.h. to her credit, with Oliver Bertram on the start line.

"Gert and Daisy," Elsie and Doris Waters, O.B.E.'s, with their Vanden Plas tourer Speed Six, registration number UW 2178 (now owned by R. S. Tubbs, Esq., O.B.E.) which they purchased especially for a Continental Tour to save breaking up the Rolls on France's pavé, here deciding their route.
Below, Jack Barclay about to give Lady Inverclyde (better known as "June", dancer and actress) a demonstration run in the 500 Miles Race winning $4\frac{1}{2}$ (YW 5758) now owned by Harry Rose, Esq.

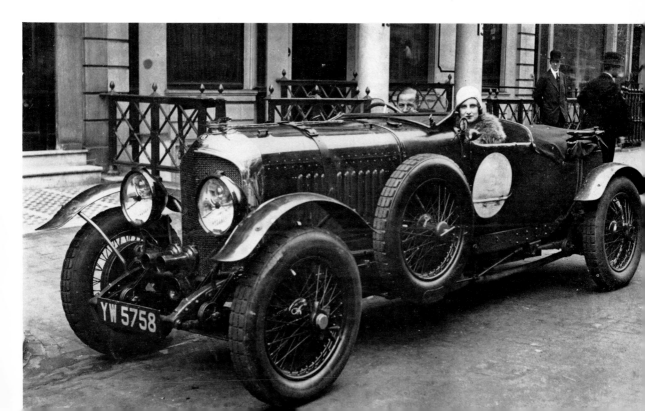

One of the few H. M. Bentley and Partner rebuilt 4½'s of 1935/36, registration number BYF 10, chassis number RN3029, here being hurled up Shelsey Hill by John im Thurn, Esq.

Lawrence Dalton at the V.S.C.C. meeting at Donington Park in 1939 with the ex-W. B. Scott 4½, registration number UU 5580 and chassis number NX3451, 1929 achievements; 11th in "Double Twelve", 8th in "6 Hours Race", 7th in "Irish G.P.", 5th in "500 Miles Race". Present owner A. A. Darling, Esq., in U.S.A.

The author having a go at the 1947 B.D.C. Silverstone meeting with the last 3 Litre made by the old company, seeing off one of the 3 Litre Sunbeams, but Anthony Heal's was ahead and uncatchable. No crash hats in those days and even the Buckinghamshire countryside looks more rural.

Sammy Davis showing he has not lost the art nor enjoyment for handling a 3 Litre Bentley at Oulton Park only recently, then I believe aged 79. The car, registration number YR 509, chassis number DE1220, now owned by Philip L. Stone, Esq.

S. C. Becker in his H. J. Mulliner coupé Speed Six frightening the marker drums at Silverstone, one of which seems to have hit back at the rear mudguard.

Below, the Hendon Police here using their own 4½ Litre Bentley, registration number GU 3063, at Goodwood while competing in a B.D.C. Eastbourne Rally, an event they twice won. The Police were always very welcome and keen participants in this once yearly fixture, which is sadly missed by many B.D.C. members from the present calendar.

The fair sex, so delightfully represented in competition by two well known competitors, Mrs. Daena Scott Brown, in the potent 4½ Litre she shares with her father Harold Pounds, here about to storm up Firle Hill.

Mrs. Brian Shoosmith (Ann, daughter of Harry Rose) dicing ever competently in her father's 1929 500 Miles Race winning car.

Most weekends see some meeting of the B.D.C. and, above, at the Ferodo Research Laboratories at Chapel-en-le-Frith is a typical gathering.

Below, Forrest Lycett in the immortal 8 Litre nearest the camera, with Gerry Crozier in the Barnato Hassan and Stanley Sedgwick in the Speed Six about to be flagged off for the standing start kilometre at Silverstone.

In Pennsylvania at Elizabethtown can be found the Klein collection of Bentleys, a few of which are seen here, Ann Klein's 3 Litre, registration number YR 5725, next to the late Sam Bailey's 4½, previously owned by the Du Pont family since new, and two Blower 4½'s, but ten yards from a positive Aladdin's cave for any Bentley enthusiast.

While below we see one of the most sporting and courageous entries of a Vintage Bentley for some time, that by Keith Schellenberg partnered by Norman Barclay and the Hon. Patrick Lindsay starting off on the London-Sydney Marathon of 1968 in Schellenberg's 8 Litre, chassis number YM5027, originally fitted with a Mulliner saloon, but now re-bodied at Nigel Arnold-Foster's workshops where the special modifications to equip her for so epic a run were also carried out.
Despite appalling bad luck in having the road crumble beneath them while halted to assist a fellow competitor who was in trouble, and having the car topple into a 20ft. ravine, she was extricated, repaired and, though out of the rally, roared on to Bombay.

F. P. Morley in his very fast 8 Litre, now registered NLH 43. This chassis, number Y R5094, has been shortened considerably from its original 13ft. wheelbase length, and below, M. L. Brewer in the late Forrest Lycett's McKenzie-prepared 4½.

Jack Sears in his father`s ex-Lycett 8 Litre hurtling up Firle Hill, and below, Sid Lawrence in the very special $4\frac{1}{2}$ he made go so rapidly.

The Bentley Drivers Club snowball run of 1962, culminating as seen here at Oulton Park, Cheshire, when well over one hundred vintage Bentleys thundered across Great Britain to commemorate the Silver Jubilee of the club. In this line up of only part of the amassed cars, at least seventy W.O. motors may be seen.

Gordon MacDonald, having just put 111.18 miles into the hour at Montlhéry, about to motor his family off, continuing their Continental holiday, and below, Gerry Crozier on the left being briefed by Geoffrey Kramer before gallantly setting out to cover the banked Montlhéry course for 50 minutes at over 120 m.p.h., a broken valve putting an end to an all but successful one hour run. The Speed Six, chassis number KF2378, registration number AC 260, is now owned by the Viscount Weir of Eastwood.

Where do all the old bodies go? With no disrespect meant to Eddie Hall enjoying himself at Oulton Park in A. R. M. Hopton's 4½, registration number BM 19, for below is the old original body off Mr. Hall's 1934 T.T. 3½ Litre Bentley, now neatly installed on a 1929 4½ competing in a South African rally. Owner B. P. Cantor.

Private club events at Silverstone always impart a happy informal atmosphere, and above we see the compulsory wheel change being effected on Gordon MacDonald's 4½ Litre during a one hour reliability run, while below, Doctor Arnold Stenhouse exercises his 4½ Litre, fitted with a boat tailed body, the property once of an Indian Potentate.

Above is the special lowered and shortened 6½ Litre devised by R. C. Moss which in 1968 recorded a timed run over the flying kilometre at 110·8 m.p.h. at Ghent, while below another 6½ Litre, this time with forward mounted radiator to obviate cutting a brand new matrix, here driven by D. O. Baker.

Above, John Hollington dices his "Le Mans" model 4½, registration number PN 3776, said to have been constructed as a spare car for the 1929 race, where its participation would almost have been superfluous, as Bentleys took the first four places that year in any case.

Below, Harry Pasco races the "Le Mans" car with special Martin Walter body to accommodate four seats on the 9ft. wheelbase version of the 3 Litre, which was entered by Scrap Thistlethwayte and Clive Gallop in the 1926 event, chassis number 1179, registration number KM 4250.

Each year there is a special Bentley invitation run at the Brighton Speed Trials and here 15 Bentleys are returning after their timed standing kilometre runs. The lower promenade driveway at this famous seaside resort provides a dramatic venue for this event, where some Bentleys' speeds at the end of the run reach around 120 m.p.h.

CHAPTER EIGHT

$3\frac{1}{2}$ LITRE

It is not intended to reiterate the already well known drama surrounding the acquisition of the assets of the old Bentley company in 1931, by Messrs. Rolls-Royce Ltd., nor to deal with the experimental supercharged "Peregrine" model, as the 18 h.p. car was known at the factory, during the period immediately after the name Bentley became a part in the production programme at Derby.

Because of the pressure from the sales department, eager to satisfy their clients' orders and the necessity for keeping alive the enormous goodwill created, a new model had to be evolved, and quickly, and as after the passage of over two years no other new Bentley was yet beyond the drawing board stage, the already well tried 18 h.p. chassis frame was offered a tuned twin carburettor version of the then current 20/25 h.p. Rolls-Royce engine.

Its success was instant, and a new form of sports car motoring had arrived.

The $3\frac{1}{2}$ Litre Bentley was first introduced to the public at Ascot in August 1933, where the press were warm in their praise for this latest Derby creation, and 1191 units of this model were made between 1933 and 1937 (the $3\frac{1}{2}$ being an alternative model still available after the introduction of the larger $4\frac{1}{4}$ Litre car.

The new Bentley of course bore no resemblance to its ancestors of the vintage years, and if critics may have decried a lower maximum speed, compared with the 8 Litre of 1931, in its defence, the ability to traverse the rapidly crowding roads of Great Britain in less time and with less effort, were points strong in its favour.

A different form of motoring had been born, and one which, the passing years have shown, has done nothing to lower the prestige of the name.

Brief Specification: $3\frac{1}{4}$in. bore $\times$ $4\frac{1}{2}$in. stroke, 3669 c.c.
6 cylinder push rod operated overhead valve engine.
Wheelbase: 10ft. 6in.
Track: 4ft. 8in.
Number of cars made: 1191.

The 3½ Litre chassis, as introduced in 1933, encouraged all coachbuilders to adopt an all enveloping tail treatment, generally incorporating a small luggage boot, which was in any case the vogue at that time. Subsequent rebuilders have found that the wide chassis frame and the rather uncompromising shape of the petrol tank and filler have complicated the more vintage approach to body design.
The price of the chassis, which included full lighting equipment and a quite comprehensive tool kit, was £1,100.

The two bodies shown here are both by Park Ward and appear to be prototypes that did not become production designs, which seems an awful shame in view of the very attractive lines of their tails and their flared mudguards.

It will be noted that stoneguards were then fitted instead of the thermostatically operated radiator shutters which became standard practice, and that eared knock-on hub caps were also employed, a feature to be found on several cars later exported abroad.

It is believed all but one of these early prototype cars were broken up, as only one, a tourer, appeared when the press were invited to the debut of the new Derby Bentley at Ascot in August 1933.

Both these motors appeared at the introduction to the press of the new Bentley in August 1933 at Ascot, although this photograph was taken outside the Aldenham House Club, Elstree, showing the Park Ward standard saloon registered ALU 323, and beyond the first production $3\frac{1}{2}$ Litre chassis number B1AE fitted with a Vanden Plas touring body and then registered ALU 321. Now with the very appropriate new registration number of RB 1933 (I have no intention of opening up the controversy over the term Rolls-Bentley) this car is owned by J. M. P. Ott, Esq., in the United States.

The success of the new Derby Bentley was well evident by the immediate queue of so many motoring sportsmen of the day, awaiting delivery. Above, Fl/Lt Staniland with his Park Ward saloon, registration number BUV 939, and below, Mr. (Wakey-Wakey) Billy Cotton, well known to Brooklands racing fans in pre-war days, also with a Park Ward saloon, registration number BUV 932.

The Duke of Richmond and Gordon, then the Earl of March, and one time apprentice at the old Bentley Works at Cricklewood, here views the engine of ALU 323 on her debut in 1933, and below at the Serpentine, Hyde Park, T. Rose-Richards is seated in a saloon whose lines have some Park Ward leanings, but differ from the production model of the time in both tail and mudguard treatment, so a I am not committing myself on the coachwork identity of AXY 746.

Earl Howe in 1934 with a standard Park Ward saloon with which he participated in a special safety first film, partly shot at Brooklands track, and below, Chairman of the old Bentley Company and director in the new concern, Woolf Barnato with his Park Ward saloon, registration number CXF 114.

E. R. Hall with his famous T.T. car here seen in its original form with coachwork by Abbott before being fitted with the two later bodies used in competition. Chassis number B35AE, registration number AXH 373 and now in Briggs Cunningham's Californian collection. Eddie Hall took second place in all three T.T. races entered by this car, finishing at the highest speeds in each event, 78.40 m.p.h. in 1934, 80.36 m.p.h. in 1935 and 80.81 m.p.h. in 1936 (using the $4\frac{1}{4}$ Litre engine that year).

Below, Captain George Eyston, one time World Land Speed Record holder, with his special light-weight two seater by Abbey Coachworks, registration number CPK 123.

Sir Roy Feddon's specially built Park Ward streamlined saloon on chassis number B189AE, registration number AXM 19, from which valuable information was compiled on reduction in wind resistance and decreased petrol consumption with increased speed, those cycle-type mudguards must have increased in unsprung front weight.

From this the production model below was evolved but retaining orthodox front mudguarding and was listed in the catalogue by Park Ward at £1,695 compared with £1,460 for their standard saloon version.

The first Hooper saloons for the $3\frac{1}{2}$ presented this appearance, this one being mounted on chassis number B129AE.

This sedanca coupé, was the first $3\frac{1}{2}$ Litre delivered to the public, a titled gentleman of note, and below, the streamlined (fast back) two door saloon by Thrupp and Maberly was to the special specification of Captain Geoffrey Smith, Editor of "The Autocar", and mounted on chassis number B67AE, registration number AXO 1, this coachwork cost £675.

The form in which the first production Park Ward saloons appeared, this one on chassis number B161AE, was probably the best selling model on the 3½, and priced at £1,460 in 1934.

It is thought only two tourers by Park Ward were constructed to this design, one appearing at the initial press showing on the 3½ Litres debut. This one on chassis number B171AE and registered AYM 223 has been in W. J. D. Roberts' family since new, though now with modified mudguarding.

Below is an H. J. Mulliner saloon on chassis number B149AE.

His Royal Highness the late Duke of Kent, father of the present Duke, was always a keen Bentley owner, and is here seen with his first 3½ Litre, chassis number B45AE, registration number AXL 1, which was later transferred to his 1936 4¼ Litre. The coachwork is by Barker and incorporates a division between front and rear compartments.

Below is a Barker Continental coupé with fixed head, on chassis number B172AH, then owned by Dr. W. F. Higgins. The recess, apparently for a folding hood, is amusing but is presumably to allow the boot lid to open fully. Registration number BEF 57.

Freestone and Webb continued the same tail treatment on their early bodies fitted to the 3½ Litre, as shown here, as had previously appeared in 1930 on the 8 Litre.

Thrupp and Maberly were responsible for this stylish special drop head coupé, thought to be a "one off" design, which was priced at £575.

This drop head coupé by H. J. Mulliner, mounted on chassis number B132AH, belonging to Ronald F. Sullivan, is a consistent concours winner in American events to the present day.

Arthur Mulliner (the other Mulliners) were responsible for this pleasing saloon on chassis number B199DK.

A page devoted to Gurney Nutting's craft. The top foursome drop head on chassis number B166DG appears to be an individual design.

The central two seater convertible was executed to order of an Indian Potentate, and the bottom sedanca model sports flared mudguards, on chassis number B199BL, unusual for this coachbuilder, and more applicable to Barker's designers.

Showing the versatility of Windovers (more often associated with limousine bodies), the top car, chassis number B131FC, is a style adopted for a series of drop heads on the Derby Bentley.

The centre car on chassis number B38DG is felt to be unique, probably executed to a client's own specification. The glamorous sedanca coupé shown at the bottom on chassis number B111FC is also probably a "one off" model, employing similar mudguarding to the coupé at the top of this page.

This two-door close coupled saloon is by Freestone and Webb on chassis number B32AH.

The Norwich coachbuilders Mann Egerton were responsible for this four-door saloon on chassis number B63AE.

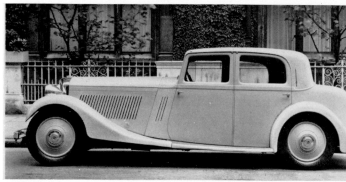

Messrs. Hooper and Co. could produce some of the best lines ever seen on some cars, but one suspects a customer's personal whim dictated this heavy tail treatment on chassis number B38DG

This two-door saloon by Mayfair on chassis number B199AE must have been an eye catcher in its day.

The old established Yorkshire coachbuilders, Rippon Bros., were responsible for this four-door saloon whose outswept bottoms to the doors imparted an individual note.

Howard "Dutch" Darrin who has injected stylish lines into coachbuilding for longer than most (1922–1968) was teamed with Fernandez of Paris, when they produced this elegant sedanca de ville on chassis number B58CR, here shown with front closed.

Scalloping was a feature of H. J. Mulliners over the years and here on chassis number B141EJ they have given this treatment to both body moulding and mudguards.

A safe, neat, conservative line was obviously Arthur Mulliner's theme in producing this four-door saloon on chassis number B84EF.

The upper sedanca coupé by Gurney Nutting on chassis number B55BL, registration number BGO 671, belongs to Donald Brown, Esq., here a concours winner at the 1964 Goodwood Pageant, and the Thrupp and Maberly version below on chassis number B143CW was exported when new to New Zealand.

The above three-position hood coupé is by Freestone Webb, while the lower coachwork is by Binder of Paris, here shown appropriately outside that fashionable restaurant Ledoyen at Les Ronds Points des Champs Elysées. The contrasting dual colour treatment and elongated bonnet strike an individual note.

This "one off" coupé by Barker now mounted on chassis number B17AE, and registered AUU 17 was originally on another 3½ Litre chassis number B178DG, both cars belonging to Hugh Curtis, Esq, She is seen here as a demonstrator at the 1964 Goodwood Pageant.

This Thrupp and Maberly drop head coupé was made to the special order of Captain Geoffrey Smith, then Editor of "The Autocar", chassis number B110BG, registration number BLK 5, now owned by K. Gates, Esq.

Four-door saloon by Arthur Mulliner on chassis number B61EJ, registration number VV 4267, displaying a moulding pattern common to all eight cars displayed on these two pages.

Arthur Mulliner adopted this bold dual colour treatment to good effect on this fast back four-door saloon, a special Motor Show exhibit, on chassis number B183BL.

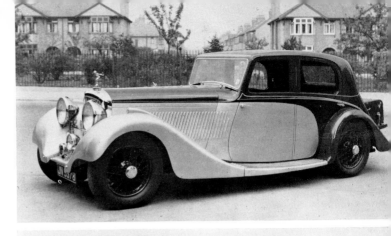

This body by Arthur Mulliner cost £465 though the specially fitted suitcases at the rear were extra; on chassis number B162DG.

Barker produced this pleasing two-door swept back saloon as a standard model, often in the company's catalogues as one of about six different listed styles available to the public. This one is mounted on chassis number B174FB.

Nicely balanced flared mudguards gave considerable character to this James Young drop head on a very early 3½ chassis as identified by the "B" on the hub caps, soon replaced by the name "Bentley".

This fixed head coupé is thought to be by the French coachbuilder Van Vooren also adopting that form of moulding accentuating the twin colour scheme.

On the right as a fast back four-door saloon by Vanden Plas on chassis number B61FC clearly showing how a recessed rear number plate would have improved the line.

Above, Arthur Mulliner favoured a rear mounted spare wheel on their swept back saloon on chassis number B159BL.

Right, William Arnold also placed the spare wheel at the rear of chassis number B171BL, a decision which often limited the luggage carrying capabilities.

A more successful attempt at streamlining by Thrupp and Maberly on chassis number B30BM with the spare wheel concealed within the boot on a sliding platform.

Thrupp and Maberly designated this two-door saloon, finished in deep red, as their "Airflow Saloon", delivered in June 1935 and registered BXY 339.

Park Ward's version of a fast back in 1934 and bearing close similarity to their show car mounted on a Rolls-Royce Phantom II, used every inch of chassis available.

The drop head coupé above is by Martin and King of Melbourne, Australia, on chassis number B83BN, the property of Dennis T. Manley, Esq., and below a very rare drop head coupé by the little known coachbuilders Corinthian Coachwork Ltd. of Kilburn.

Three drop head coupés, all of French origin. That shown above is by Kellner on chassis number B59CW, who saw no need for running boards on so low a car.

Here, one of the very few bodies by Antem of Paris mounted on a Bentley chassis, this one number B24BN and registered BLO 34, though destined for U.K., retained her Marchal head lamps as evidence of her birth place, while below another Kellner body, on chassis B31BL, retained rather Anglicized lines but is given away by that exposed name plate at the scuttle bottom.

The boot shape of this very attractive drop head is typical of the rounded style adopted by Thrupp and Maberly between 1932 and 1937, before their semi-razor-edge form supplemented this pattern.

Two drop head coupés by Hooper, both, it is thought, "one off" designs, the photographer obviously favoured a specially chosen site. The lower body is mounted on chassis number B198AH.

This special four-door saloon by Park Ward, which dispensed with central pillars above the waist line, was termed "Californian Top Saloon".

Both these bodies were executed by Park Ward, the drop head coupé above was their standard model, the complete car costing £1,485, and displays their flush line with hood folded.

The coachwork below mounted on chassis number B135EJ was their special coupé de ville constructed for the 1935 Motor Show at Olympia, and is thought to be unique.

The coachbuilder Plaxton of Scarborough was responsible for this four-door saloon on chassis number B90CR.

The bold lining on this Vanden Plas pillarless saloon mounted on chassis number B63EJ accentuated its elegance.

Showing the practical nature of Vanden Plas pillarless construction on chassis number B33EJ.

Mann Egerton produced this neat four-door model on chassis number B151EJ.

This compact two-door saloon by Mayfair is mounted on chassis number B88EF.

Gurney Nutting produced this exotic coupé on chassis number B183EJ, for an Indian Maharajah in whose household it remained until recently acquired by Major F. H. Moore in Calcutta.

Salmons built this "one off" design for S. E. Sears, Esq., and her elegant lines earned her the title of Champion car at the 1935 Eastbourne Rally, registration number VV 2683.

The Carlton Carriage Company fitted this all-weather body to chassis number B83CW.

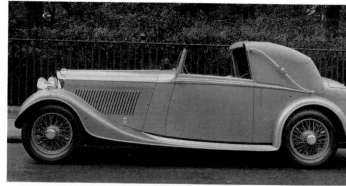

The luggage boot shape is the best clue to this coachbuilder's identity, Messrs. Thrupp and Maberly on chassis number B58EF.

This Barker two-seater drop head coupé is thought to be an individual design on chassis number B134EF.

A drop head by H. J. Mulliner on chassis number B168AH and registered BGO 288.

This fixed head sedanca coupé on chassis number B65DK is possibly a "one off" by Thrupp and Maberly.

Another style from those Norwich coachbuilders, Mann Egerton.

Freestone and Webb produced this saloon on chassis number B8AH.

Arthur Mulliner who were responsible for this saloon on chassis number B149CW appear to have dispensed with running boards.

Another style from Hoopers who specialised more in client's individual wishes than many coachbuilders.

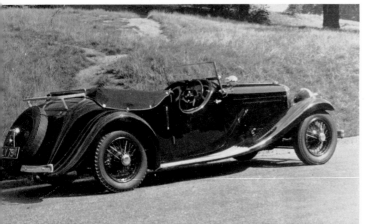

The upper body on chassis number B11 AE has been constructed by the owner, C. B. D. Sargeant. Registration number AXX 286. The centre coachwork is by Gurney Nutting, chassis number B127 BL, registration number BLY 794, owned by Mr. Marshall Stuart in New Zealand. This rear decked tourer with screens to protect the rear occupants, is by Freestone and Webb on chassis number B198CR, registered in UK as BXN 401, and now owned by Lt. Col. H. W. Taylor.

In the 30's one could still order coachwork to one's own specification and doubtless Freestone and Webb supplied this special two-seater to a client's own ideas on chassis number B94EF.

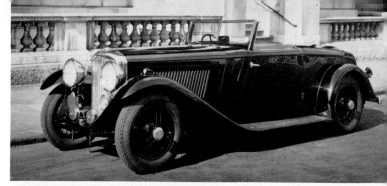

Although this individual tourer is attributed to the American coachbuilder Derham, and fitted to chassis number B203EJ, it started life as a Vanden Plas tourer supplied to the Du Pont family. Derham remodelled it, and while visiting England in 1939 it became interned for the Duration and was registered as FXE9. The Du Ponts retained her until 1946.

I think I know outside which Stately Northumberland Home this picture was taken, I think I know the owner, but the coachbuilder's name defies me, other than a guess at Vanden Plas.

However, there are no doubts about this concours winning all-weather tourer by Vanden Plas to Oxborrow and Fuller's specification and registered BLY 4. A classic design repeated with slight restyling until 1939. This particular car featured in numerous rallies as indicated by some of her displayed trophies.

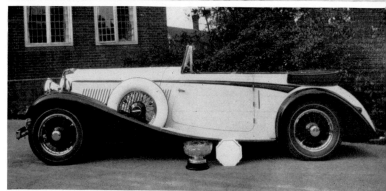

The name of Mann Egerton has long been associated with the motor industry and appropriately enough, this drop head coupé bears the Norfolk registration number of NG 7438, as testimony to its birthplace.

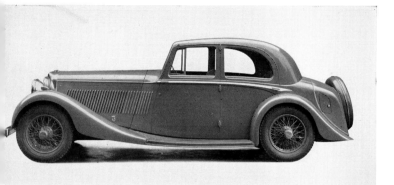

This was Barker's special design for the 1935 Scottish Motor Show, fitted to chassis number B22FB.

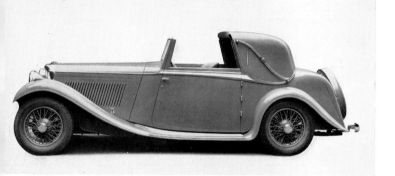

Another show car, this time a sedanca coupé on chassis number B19BN and displayed on the Barker stand in 1934.

With variations to the mudguarding this was Barker's standard drop head coupé form, fitted to chassis number B112AH.

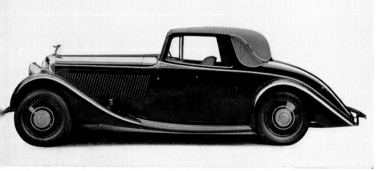

Sir F. Sanderson, Bart., commissioned this special Barker close coupled fixed head coupé fitted to chassis number B67DK, though it appears this baronet had strong Rolls-Royce leanings, judging by the radiator mascot.

` This page is devoted to the craft of James Young, all of individual design. The top four-seater drop head is fitted to chassis number ` B3CW.

The customer who decreed this two-seater drop head coupé appears to have desired ample luggage accommodation and adequate warning of approach, judging from the special horn arrangement.

This neat two-seater, however, made provision for additional passengers in the dickey seat, fitted to chassis number B39BL, and fortunately survives today in a most attractive two-colour scheme.

Of rather more orthodox form, this four-some drop head coupé was fitted to chassis B157CW and bravely scorned the need for bumpers.

Above, a drop head coupé by Messrs. Windovers fitted to chassis number B22AH.

This special four door all-weather body is by Salmons on chassis number B37EJ.

Below is another Windovers drop head coupé, this time incorporating a concealed hood when folded down within the body sides.

CHAPTER NINE

4¼ LITRE

In March of 1936 the larger 4¼ Litre engine became available, still employing exactly the same chassis, gear box and back axle ratios, as used in the 3½ Litre car.·

The enlarged unit gave about the same acceleration figures in top as had been given by the 3½ in third, but otherwise performance differed but little. Both motors, of exactly the same design and appearance (if one discounts the larger air filter silencer fitted to the twin S.U. carburettors), could easily top 90 m.p.h., but neither could quite reach the magic "100" in completely standard form, unless aided by favourable circumstances.

Eddie Hall's famous "TT" car of three consecutive years (1934-1936) could achieve around 120 m.p.h. fully extended, and the almost equally well known ex-Embiricos streamlined Van Vooren saloon of Monthlery fame, could just about equal this figure (114 miles in the hour being fair indication of her capabilities).

However it was not just speed that provided the great appeal of these cars, it was the extreme silence and freedom from drama that characterised this new era of fast effortless motoring.

For the statistically minded 1241 4¼ Litres were produced between March 1936 and about May 1939 when the last overdrive chassis were completed, though many MX series cars were of course bodied well after that date.

At this time in the year motor companies had to plan for the forthcoming October Motor Show and the new (Next Year's) models. For 1940 the Mark V, front independently sprung car, was then already being developed.

With the introduction of the overdrive series gear box in late 1938 employing a 4.3 to 1 rear axle, compared with the earlier standard 4.1 to 1 ratio, modifications were also made to the camshaft, which had less overlap in its latest form, and further added to the difficulty of overdriving the car, a danger recently arising out of the newly constructed fast European motorways, a contingency the company were at pains to obviate, and as a result one of the most pleasing pre-war touring cars was evolved.

Brief Specification: 3½in. bore × 4½in. stroke, 4257 c.c.

6 cylinder push rod operated overhead valve engine.

Wheelbase: 10ft. 6in.

Track: 4ft. 8in.

Number of cars made: 1241.

A James Young saloon on chassis number B111LE owned by R. G. Lawrence, Esq., in British Columbia, displaying a style reminiscent of the earlier Humber Vogue, and the cars below show variations on this theme.

Gurney Nutting's version on chassis number B180JD, registration number DGP 227 and owned by Steve Morton of Illinois.

Below, Barker's interpretation on chassis number B12GA.

Spats for the rear mudguard became fashionable about 1936-37, and here Barker have dressed theirs up in decorative and somewhat complicated style.

Above, a flamboyant offering by the Carlton Carriage Co. on chassis number B203KU which was of pillarless construction.
Below, Vanden Plas have executed a unique two door saloon with very pleasing lines on chassis number B128KT, registration number EMY4, and winner of 'The Motor' Trophy at the 1938 Eastbourne Concours.

Another "one off" by the Carlton Carriage Co. for Offord & Sons on chassis number B56JD, an all-weather phaeton incorporating a rear screen. The back mudguard spats have been removed in this view. Owner, James P. Smith, Esq.

Windovers styling for a special all-weather tourer with extra luggage carrying facilities on the boot, on chassis number B80MR.

The top car is by Hooper with concealed hood beneath that rear decking, finished in Royal Blue and Black.

Above, Vanden Plas demonstrate their mastery in keeping a low folded hood line in this four door version of their all-weather tourer on chassis number B72JD, owned as shown here by The Earl of Gosford. Below, Thrupp and Maberly's phaeton on chassis B137LE frankly had a neater line with the hood raised.

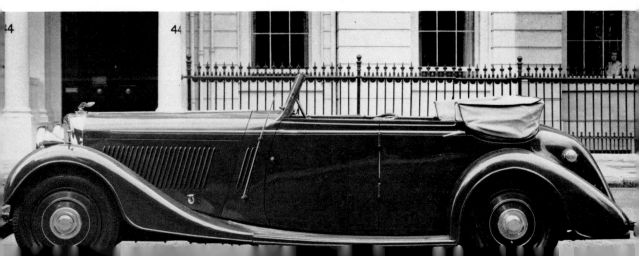

The top fixed head coupé by Freestone and Webb, on chassis number B12HK, has unusual cut-away running board treatment.

This unique Continental styling comes from Vesters and Neirinck of Brussels on chassis number B156KT, owned by C. R. Lang, Esq. The optional eared knock on hub caps so often used on export cars, will be noticed.

Nicknamed the "Honeymoon Express", this was Park Ward's special show car at Earls Court in 1938, mounted on chassis number B30MR and registered FLU 663 she is now owned by M. A. Richmond, Esq.

This H. J. Mulliner coupé is believed to be a "one off" design, seating three persons, the rear member crosswise, on a single folding seat, or alternatively affording additional luggage space for the grand tour.

This fixed head coupé, which would these days probably be called a "hard top", does give the appearance that the front half might be in sedanca form. Coachwork by H. J. Mulliner, on chassis number B114GA.

Freestone and Webb specialised in razor-edge styling which earned the description of "Top Hat", but this is the only known two door version on a 4¼, chassis number B147HM, registered DLA 379, and now owned by R. F. Baldwin, Esq.

A Freestone and Webb two door four light saloon on chassis B36JD.

This fixed head coupé by Park Ward, mounted on chassis number B38KT, has opening panels to the bonnet instead of the customary louvres.

Above, one of the most popular styles by Vanden Plas, their two door all-weather body so often successful in Concours d'Elegances. This shot of CLW 44 is one of the numerous official company photographs of this car.
Below, with typical Teutonic hood line this coupé by Erdmann & Rossi of Berlin is mounted on chassis number B58LS, now owned by Mr. Cronckhite in California.

Three views showing the very neat stowage of the disappearing hood by H. J. Mulliner under the rear square edged folding panel, a feature common to this coachbuilder during the period 1935-39.
This particular car is thought to be the 1939 car registered FLH 777 and a participent in that year's R.A.C. Brighton Rally.

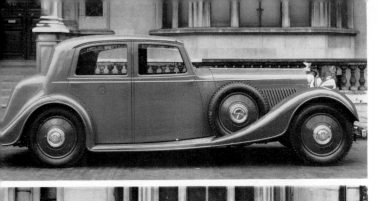

Thrupp and Maberly evolved an extremely clean line with their semi razor-edge treatment in 1936, as shown here on chassis B173HM, which supplemented their earlier more rounded coachwork.

James Young must have produced more individual styles than many body builders, and this saloon on chassis number B71MX is unique, to my knowledge.

Salmons, well known for their Tickford folding head conversions, also found time to produce individual coachwork, and this saloon is an example.

This airflow saloon by Gurney Nutting, on chassis B118HK, exemplifies the rather conservative approach to streamlining felt appropriate for such high class vehicles.
Registration number DXN 401.

Typically H. J. Mulliner. This form often incorporating their perspex roof panels to increase visibility, displays perfect taste and an excellent line.

The mudguard treatment of this model, on chassis number B162LS, is a good clue to the originator, Messrs. Gurney Nutting.

Park Ward produced more saloon bodies on the Derby chassis than any other coach-builder, and this version is their Continental model with special mudguarding and side mounted spare wheel, distinguishing it from the more usual standard steel saloon.

Another different style from James Young, on chassis B183GP, with semi recessed rear mounted spare wheel.

This coachwork by Park Ward, seems to incorporate styling differing from either of their two more familiar saloon models.

Another razor-edged saloon, this time by Mann Egerton, on chassis number B115MX, just fails to capture the panache of other champions of this style. Registration number FLX 800.

This open two seater tourer by Carlton mounted on chassis number B55KU and registered FPJ 100 competed in the R.A.C. Blackpool Rally and the J.C.C. Brooklands Rally in 1939.

This special coupé, shown above, was constructed by Hoopers for H. Von Berge and registered DXV 69. Below is possibly one of the most pleasing drop heads ever designed by Vanden Plas. This was their special 1938 Scottish Motor Show exhibit, employing the same mudguard treatment as their 1938 Earls Court Show sports tourer. Mounted on chassis number B106MR and registered HPC 3.

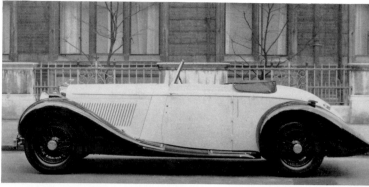

The Carlton Carriage Company produced this special drop head coupé on chassis number B44MR, which appears to have retained the then rather dated dickey seat.

This Vanden Plas two seater appears to be a "one off" design mounted on chassis number B196HK, and from the steps on the rear, mudguards would also seem to be fitted with dickey seat, or rumble seat, as termed across the Atlantic.

James Young were responsible for this striking open two seater sports model with concealed hood and large rear luggage locker. Chassis number B31LE.

Vanden Plas are credited with this concealed hood drop head, on chassis number B97GP, whose scalloped side panels are more in accord with H. J. Mulliner practice.

Sedanca coupés all. The top one is by H. J. Mulliner on chassis number B92GA and though, in common with most Derby cars of this era, the boot held very little, the added luggage grid does nothing for her lines.

The centre version is by James Young mounted on chassis number B174KT, while the lower glamorous model will be familiar to B.D.C. members both sides of the Atlantic. Bob Hicks' Gurney Nutting concours winning car on chassis number B188MR, registration number 514 BPL.

H. J. Mulliner's peculiar treatment of the moulding around the boot is again evident here on chassis number B79MX owned by J. B. Allen, Esq.

The edition above cannot be definitely identified. The hood arrangement is rather heavier than the other sedanca coupés depicted here.
Below is the parallel opening door sedanca coupé by James Young, so often displayed in pre-war official advertisements, on chassis B39LE and registered EXO 5. Now owned by Lennox C. Bauer, Jnr.

Messrs Vanden Plas (England) 1923 Ltd. used two standard forms for their open sports 4 seater tourers on the 4¼ Litre. That shown above was the style introduced for 1938 and it is thought only three were constructed, one being retained and mounted on Rusty Russ-Turner's 1939 overdrive chassis, while below is the form more familiar and presumably more popular, as exemplified by Sir Malcolm Campbell's 1936 model (shown here), registration number CXK 1, chassis number B109KU, now owned by William R. Johnson in Rhode Island. About 8 of this version were fitted to 4¼'s in 1936-1937, and with some minor styling changes this form was reintroduced for 1939 and mounted on one 1938 LE series chassis and three 1939 overdrive models.

This body reported to be by Vanden Plas looks more Corsica in style, and certainly is a form unknown to the author. Chassis number B79JY, registration number DYH 820, the property of M. W. P. Cripps, Esq.

Below is the unique torpedo tourer by Vesters & Neirinck here seen at the 1964 Goodwood Pageant, then owned by Major Floor. The eared knock-on hubs are again in evidence. This car, registration number 4183 AD, mounted on chassis number B24LS was recently auctioned at Sotheby's and is now owned by John C. North, Esq.

This Park Ward body on chassis number B51MX, registration number FYL 7, shown above, is the version known as their Continental Saloon, owned by Dr. Eustace Hope, while below, also by Park Ward, is their razor-edged edition mounted on chassis number B54MR, registration number FLB 356, owned by Harold Hinchcliffe, Esq.

H. J. Mulliner's "High Vision" saloon with their special Perspex roof panels and quarter lights brought well back at the rear on chassis B102MR.

The very neat 2 door saloon shown above is by James Young on chassis number B139MX, a premier concours winner at its first appearance, while below is Windover full length saloon on chassis number B123MX designed to provide extra space in the rear compartment.

The drop head body shown above, by Vanden Plas, cost £525 and differed from their standard version in the treatment of the rear boot lid. Their flush folding hood line is well exemplified here.

Above, mounted on chassis number B26MR, is Hooper's styling for a drop head. Registered KYR 496, this car is now owned by J. B. Archibald, Esq. While below is a special "one off" design executed by Vanden Plas to a client's own specification to provide exceptional luggage accommodation for two on tour, with twin folding transverse occasionals behind the front bench seat. Registration number ELB 3.

In the 30's, there were about forty coachbuilders still producing individual bodies, and these four drop head coupés were but a few of those available. That shown at the top is by Mayfair on chassis number B203GP.

The Carlton Carriage Company produced this model on chassis number B76KT.

The falling waistline was a feature often seen, and used here by Windovers on chassis number B41MX.

If there is any similarity to the larger M.G.s of the period, this is accounted for by the coachwork being by Salmons, who produced similar bodies for the Abingdon-based company.

Both these coupés are by Erdmann and Rossi of Berlin, the upper one displaying the usual problem experienced with most heavily padded hoods, that of folding it down to present a low line, while the lower car, apparently with sedanca front, has mudguarding extremely reminiscent of Gurney Nutting lines.

The top Sedanca de Ville, a rare body style on the Derby Bentley, is by Park Ward, and at present owned by Ronald Westall, Esq., the chauffeur's compartment here being shown in covered form.

James Young are the coach-builders responsible for this model, known as a Brougham. This rare two door body is on chassis number B38MR.

Another special two door saloon by James Young, this model on chassis number B100MR, however, refrains from adopting the raised panel styling of the model shown above.

The bottom car was H. J. Mulliner's special show car at Earls Court in 1938, featuring semi razor-edge treatment and incorporating that coachbuilder's special transparent perspex panels in the roof above the front passengers. Present owner Dr. C. E. Evans. Chassis number B28MR, registered FGT 867.

This special close coupled saloon was executed by H. J. Mulliner to the design of R. G. McLeod, Esq., on chassis number B142MR, in 1939; raced by Eric Forrest-Greene in the Argentine after World War II, and now owned by Dr. Regules in Montevideo.

This saloon by H. J. Mulliner was constructed in about 1948, for a 1937 4¼ Litre chassis, and the resemblance to their 1939 Mark V car, which should have appeared at that year's Motor Show, will be apparent (see page 235).

Freestone and Webb's razor edge styling is beautifully displayed here on chassis number B144JD and registered in U.K. as DXE 44, now the property of N. W. Stickney, Esq., in the United States.

Though Park Ward produced a swept back saloon like the one depicted here, those boot lid catches and mudguard shaping bear the hall mark of Thrupp and Maberly, and it is these coachbuilders who, I feel, are responsible for this body.

It is thought the same designers had a hand in all three Sedanca coupés shown here. Left, one by Gurney Nutting, is mounted on chassis number B70KT.

Above, a strong Gallic influence has crept into this edition, also by Gurney Nutting, on chassis number B166JD and registered EGH 511. Left, this particular boot shape could only emanate from James Young, who amalgamated with Gurney Nutting in the Jack Barclay empire. This one was mounted on chassis B86MR.

Three convertibles. The top one by Park Ward, was their 1938 Earls Court show car, on chassis number B16MR, registered EYX 399, and now owned by T. Reich, Esq. On the right, on chassis number B29GP, a James Young body, and below, on chassis number B42MR, Vanden Plas built their traffic indicators into the doors, an unusual procedure.

All drop heads—that shown above, by Gurney Nutting, on chassis number B202GA favoured the three position hood form.

Frankly I don`t know who made the one above, on chassis number B81HM, but would toss a coin between Park Ward and Vanden Plas; but the body below, on chassis number B109LE, is by Thrupp and Maberly.

This impeccably turned out Park Ward coupé, though apparently a perfectly standard example, was first commissioned by Baron Rothschild who failed to take delivery and she was acquired new by the present owner's father.

After several subsequent owners, she crossed the Atlantic and from the U.S.A. Richard Broster tracked her down to bring her back to the family, and restore her to "as new" order again.

Chassis number B2HK, registration number CKA 920, this motor cost £1,535 new in 1936 and was undoubtedly one of the most popular drop head coupé bodies available on the Derby Bentley.

Vanden Plas's show car for Earls Court 1938. Chassis number B20MR and registered EOM 560, this car is owned by R. C. Robertson, Esq.

Specially constructed by Thrupp and Maberly for Capt. Geoffrey Smith of The Autocar, this beautiful three position hood coupé was mounted on chassis number B137KU and then registered EME5. Now re-registered as GTU 311, she belongs to D. F. Lecket, Esq. Also by Thrupp and Maberly is their semi-razor edged saloon for 1938/39.

The Duke of Kent, father of the present Duke, had Hooper make this partitioned sports saloon for his 4¼ chassis number B142HK, (now belonging to P. W. R. Ball, Esq.) transferring the plates (registration number AXL 1) from his similar Barker bodied 3½ Litre, and below, also by Hooper, is their semi razor-edge design on chassis number B134MR, registration number FYU 805 belonging to J. S. F. Gallant, Esq.

Above, is a rare two door tourer by Cockshoot, on chassis number B186JD, with hood concealed in a well at the back of the body, and on the left, a two door saloon by Thrupp and Maberly, mounted on an overdrive series, chassis number B179MX.

Edmunds Metal Works, of Plymouth, evolved this very fine tourer for Dr. Eustace Hope on chassis number B63MX, registration number FYW 822, which has much in common with the lines of the 1938 design by Vanden Plas.

Above, Henry Wilkins looks justifiably proud of his Kensington Gardens class winner for 1966. Constructed by Abbey Panels Ltd., to Mr. Wilkins's own design, this two seater is mounted on chassis number B180LS, registration number ENC 619.

This very racey-looking two seater, shortened and lowered with competition in view, is fitted to chassis number B66GA, and registered SY 5858, the property of A. J. Rivers Fletcher, Esq., she originally bore a Hooper saloon body.

Two different approaches in quest of a sportier line. That above is by P. A. M. Page, and now owned by J. A. Stevens, on chassis number B191JY, registration number DXW 654, employing the welded steel frame method of construction and content with two seats only, while that below, by the author, using the traditional ash frame method with aluminium panelling on chassis number B198LS, registration number BGG 842, and owned by W. P. Kimberley, Esq., has been designed as a two plus two torpedo.

The car above has often erroneously been dubbed "The Corniche", whereas actually she is a 1938 model, chassis number B27LE, with numerous departures from standard specification to the special order of Mr. Sleater, representative for Rolls-Royce France, for the famous Greek racing driver Mr. Embiricos and endowed with this streamlined saloon by Van Vooren of Paris to Paulin's design. Three times entrant for post-war "Le Mans" races, driven by her owner Soltan Hay, she covered 114 miles in the hour at Brooklands in 1939 driven by Capt. George Eyston.

Below is similar coachwork produced by Van Vooren, on chassis number B29LE, though retaining the traditional Bentley radiator in lieu of the other cars' cowled front. This car has been owned by the Garthwaite family in New York since new.

CHAPTER TEN

MARK V AND CORNICHE

Two different models were envisaged for Bentley's production for 1940. The Mark V incorporating independent front suspension for the first time on a Bentley and retaining an overdrive gear box, similar to the previous "M" series, but now equipped with the added advantage of synchromesh on 2nd gear as well as the upper ratios. This model was intended for touring, and larger saloon coachwork. The Corniche version, with an alternative close ratio gearbox, and lighter disc bolt-on wheels, was designed for high speed (110 m.p.h.) with aerodynamic bodies in mind. It is lamentable that the only two Corniches made should have been destroyed by enemy action in Europe, while waiting shipment back to England.

The engines for both models were overhead valve push rod units of 4,257 c.c., possibly bearing closer resemblance to the 30 h.p. Rolls-Royce Wraith of the time than the current $4\frac{1}{4}$ Litre Bentley power plant.

A divided propellor shaft, to avoid any possibility of vibration, was used in the extremely stiff cross-braced chassis frame.

It is believed that a batch of 35 chassis were originally sanctioned up to chassis number B70AW, but the intervention of war in 1939 stopped production, and probably not more than 17 cars were actually completed, some of which were appropriated by important service and ministerial personages, amongst them Earl Howe and Bomber Harris, for active war-time use.

With the difficulty later over the availability of spares for these cars, some were dismantled, and ownership of the few remaining was a jealously guarded matter of policy by the company for some time.

Possibly only seven now exist, but having had the good fortune to have sampled a really excellent specimen, I can say that this undoubtedly was one of the most pleasant Bentleys to drive ever constructed, and this statement is made with daily experience of an early light 'R' Type Continental for comparison.

It is regrettable that this little known model never reached the public in any numbers, as it was several years ahead of its time.

Brief Specification: $3\frac{1}{2}$ in. bore x $4\frac{1}{2}$ in. stroke, 4,257 c.c.
6 cylinder o.h.v. push rod operated engine.
Wheelbase: 10 ft. 4 in.
Track: (Front) 4 ft. $8\frac{1}{4}$ in.
(Rear) 4 ft. 10 in.

Number of cars made: Possibly 17.

Right, this picture of the Mark V engine clearly shows the difference between its layout and that of the earlier 4¼ Litre unit. The distributor on the nearside and the slightly different shaped exhaust manifold and water pump at the rear, while below it will be seen that the intake from the twin S.U. carburettors to the air filter has also been changed from the previous design.

Above, the stiff cruciform braced frame will be noted to differ from the previous Bentley practice, and the innovation of the divided propellor shaft is displayed. A new shaped petrol tank of 16 gallon capacity is fitted further inboard, while on the right, similarity to the post war Mark VI front independent suspension is evident.

Destined for display at the Paris Salon (a show always preceding our own motor show) this drop head coupé, with three position hood by Saoutchik, was fitted to chassis number B14AW, the seventh production Mark V. From her appearance, when imported back from France into U.K., soon after the war then finished in black with white twill hood, she seemed to have been carefully stored and to have survived the intervening seven years without blemish. Her registration number MXT 3 remained with her until shipment to the United States in about 1967, repainted grey with matching hood material, to become the possession of Thomas J. Bahr, in California.

This is probably the only open Mark V in existence though Park Ward did fit at least one drop head coupé body to a Mark V chassis, which was used by Bomber Harris, but it was found to lack the rigidity imparted by the saloon coachwork, and I believe later dismantled.

The Park Ward saloon shown above at the 1964 Goodwood Pageant, registered GGO 185 and fitted to chassis number B16AW, is now smartly painted in primrose and black, and owned by Michael Ellman-Brown. It was originally Woolf Barnato's own personal car. Below, a prototype model with coachwork also by Park Ward, on experimental chassis number 1BV, and fitted with the lighter Sankey pressed steel disc bolt-on wheels, as used on the Corniche model. The similarity to the post war Mark VI standard steel saloon is very apparent.

This standard Park Ward saloon, registration number RC 7477, has coachwork similar to that fitted to the experimental chassis number 11BV (which had the registration number RC 7420) later to be equipped with the post war eight cylinder Rolls-Royce unit and nicknamed the "Scalded Cat", a model which never saw series production, Below, this beautiful H. J. Mulliner semi razor-edge saloon, fitted to chassis number B30AW, was intended for display at the 1939 Motor Show at Earls Court. It later became the personal transport of Mr. Llewellyn-Smith of Rolls-Royce. The registration number is now GJ 88 and is owned by Michael Ellman-Brown. The close resemblance to the coachwork fitted post war to a 1937 $4\frac{1}{4}$ Litre chassis (see page 220) is obvious.

"The Corniche". Here are the only known official photographs existing of this exciting car. It is thought two were constructed and dispatched to the continent for testing in August 1939, from whence, unfortunately they were never destined to return. The one seen here, registration number GRA 270, was destroyed by enemy action on the quayside at Dieppe, her keys eventually being returned by the R.A.C., the only material evidence now of her existance. Her experimental chassis number was 14BV, and the coachwork was by Van Vooren. The stream-lined frontal design must have caused some consternation amongst the diehard traditionalists at Derby and Conduit Street but such an approach was in keeping with the general concept and purpose for which this model was intended, that of fast travel with the least possible effort and noise.

Not the happiest of lines aesthetically, perhaps, but clearly showing the forward thinking of the development and research division.

CHAPTER ELEVEN

THE SILENT SPORTS CAR

This was the advertising slogan which heralded the arrival of the new Bentley from Derby in 1933, and anyone witnessing the epic drives of Eddie Hall in the three Tourist Trophy races of 1934-1936 and later in the post war Le Mans of 1950 with the same car, and Soltan Hay's entry in three completely trouble-free consecutive Le Mans races in the 1938 ex Embiricos car, with 6th place in 1948, would never question the accuracy of this description. Sports car it truly is, albeit a very docile and impeccably mannered one.

Being fortunate enough to have two open models of the $4\frac{1}{4}$ Litre version, I feel justified after seventeen years' experience of this model, to express the view that the Derby car is really a very refined vintage motor. The engine is of course, a direct development of the 20 h.p. Rolls-Royce unit of 1923, and the chassis destined for the still-born 18 h.p. machine of around 1930, known at the works as the "Peregrine", owes nothing in its design to modern trends. With its old-fashioned cart springs all round, a lightened edition with hydraulic shock absorbers adjusted accordingly, gives the most delightful, responsive, taut ride imaginable.

If it can be critised as a competition machine in any way, it might be in respect of the axle ratios. From 1933 to 1938, a 4.1 to 1 ratio was employed (except for a very few of the alternative special 3.9 versions) which resulted in reaching the red sector on the revolution counter at 4,500 r.p.m. all too readily on any reasonable straight stretch, this being the equivalent to about 95 m.p.h. The overdrive gearbox using a 4.3 back end with an overdrive 4th speed of 3.64 to 1, allows effortless 90 m.p.h. cruising at 3,000 revs in the geared up top cog, though utterly precludes achieving the theoretical maximum of around 110 m.p.h. at 3,600, at which figure this series peaks. Having tuned both forms of $4\frac{1}{4}$ engine to approximately the same degree, with a view to greater efficiency, without sacrificing in any degree the flexibility and smoothness for which these machines are renowned, I can quote these figures with some authority.

However, far more able pens than mine have stated it is more the manner in which this performance is delivered than the actual speeds achieved that endears these motors to their owners.

Possibly no greater champion of the Derby car exists than Rusty Russ-Turner, whose twin supercharged $4\frac{1}{4}$ made fastest Bentley time at both Brighton and Firle Hill Climb in the same year, competing against the hottest winged "B" machinery of all decades, further strengthening its right to be included among that exclusive circle of Sports Cars.

Here again in 1936, at the Ards Circuit, E. R. Hall leads the Hon. Brian Lewis (now Lord Essendon) in his 4½ Litre Lagonda, reliving their epic duel of 1934, when both were driving the same makes of car. For the third time in succession (using race number 7 each year) Eddie Hall finished the Tourist Trophy at the highest speed, mostly in torrential rain.

In 1935, E. R. Hall used the same four seater coachwork, as employed in 1934, necessitated by the A1 regulations at that time, but with more elegant streamlined mudguards. The compression ratio was raised to 8.35 to 1 and the output was said to be 152 b.h.p. Below, still employing the same chassis number B35AE, Eddie Hall, in 1936, installed a $4\frac{1}{4}$ Litre engine of 163 b.h.p. and a new two seater body with better aerodynamic lines, in which form this famous car still exists to-day with Briggs Cunningham in California.

You cannot keep a good dog down. Above, Eddie Hall tops up the spare oil reservoir on the 1934 T.T. car, chassis number B35AE, during the 1950 Le Mans race, in which he finished in eighth place after a solo drive. The scene here typifies the tense atmosphere surrounding a pit stop in this exciting event. Below, the Bentley is seen at a point on this famous circuit known so well from previous Le Mans' history to so many, White House 23 years on.

From the early Le Mans days the entry of Bentleys in competition has ever been the field for private enthu-
siasts, and above, a victorious 4¼ Litre is seen at the termination of the Lisbon Rally, in which it was driven
by Jorge de Melo e Fraro (Conde de Monte Real).

Below, Jack Evan Cook drifts his James Young two seater drop head coupé through the first bend of Firle
Hill. This motor, registration number CXB 277, now forms part of the Bentley stable of that keen motoring
vicar, the Rev. H. I. Noakes, whose Bentley collection also includes vintage specimens of the marque.

The late Lord Ebury, is here seen pressing on up Prescott Hill in the Abbott bodied 3½ Litre, chassis number B43AE, registered AXY666, now owned by Lord Doune.

Fastest Bentley at both Brighton Speed Trials and Firle Hill in the same year, here Rusty Russ-Turner winds up his twin supercharged 4¼ Litre, chassis number B16KT and registered DYV289, with special two seater coachwork by Caffyns.

Both these 4¼ Litres were devised by P. A. M. Page. That nearest the camera, chassis number B109MX, registered 5960PH, is driven by its creator at Brighton. His earlier car, chassis number B191JY and registered DXW654, is now owned by O. S. Pattison, and displays the accelerative advantage of the earlier gear box over the overdrive type, but for high speed cruising on the Autostrada del Sole it would be a different matter.

CHAPTER TWELVE

MARK VI AND 'R' TYPE

With the return of peace, the Rolls-Royce company transferred its motor division, previously situated at Derby, to its Crewe factory, and for the first time embarked upon the production of complete cars, the bodywork having been left always before to individual coachbuilders.

The first new Bentley for 1946 was the Mark VI, employing similar independent front suspension to its pre-war sister the Mark V, but using an overhead inlet, side exhaust valve layout for the cylinder head, not so dissimilar to that of the ill-fated 4 Litre of 1931.

The standard steel body also would appear to have derived much of its appearance from the Park Ward saloon fitted to the Mark V in 1939.

Between 1946 and 1951 the engine size remained the same as the capacity of the pre-war car at 4,257 c.c., to be increased to 4,566 c.c. for the 1952 models, and the term "big bore small boot" soon became accepted as a description for a much sought after model.

The same larger engine was installed into the 'R' Type chassis for 1954, and though the wheelbase remained the same at 10 ft., the chassis length was increased to accommodate the larger rear boot, and an automatic gearbox became optional.

If policy had so far indicated the desirability for a basically family type motor, in 1951 the prototype Continental model was born, to create a furore in the motor industry when it was announced in 1953. Once again a motor with performance in line with the name had been created. Here was a 120 m.p.h. motor, at least in the earlier lighter versions, that would return better than 20 m.p.g. and whose four passengers travelled in near utter silence, if the windows were kept closed.

H. J. Mulliner, now part of the Rolls-Royce empire, were responsible for these fast back streamline saloons, whose aerodynamic lines were only infringed upon by the degree of conservatism expected of it by its clientele, demanding that the traditional Bentley radiator should be retained in front. The Corniche approach of 1940 was not to be tolerated.

Though first produced with a 4.5 litre capacity engine, this in 1955 became enlarged to 4.9 litres in which form it remained until superseded by the 'S' Series.

The 'R' Type Continental became a classic in its own time, and a collector's piece without experience of which no connoisseur of motoring can consider his life complete.

Brief Specification: **Mark VI** ($4\frac{1}{4}$ Litre) $3\frac{1}{2}$ in. bore $\times 4\frac{1}{2}$ in. stroke, 4,257 c.c.
($4\frac{1}{2}$ Litre) $3\frac{5}{8}$ in. bore $\times 4\frac{1}{2}$ in. stroke, 4,566 c.c.
Six cylinder push rod o/h inlet side exhaust valve engine.
Wheelbase: 10 ft.
Track: 4 ft. $8\frac{1}{2}$ in. front. 4 ft. $10\frac{1}{2}$ in. rear.
'R' Type (4.5 Litre) $3\frac{5}{8}$ in. bore $\times 4\frac{1}{2}$ in. stroke, 4.566 c.c.
(4.9 Litre) $3\frac{3}{4}$ in. bore $\times 4\frac{1}{2}$ in. stroke, 4,887 c.c.
Chassis dimensions the same as for the Mark VI.
Number of cars made: Mark VI, 4,946. 'R' Type, 2,320. 'R' Type Continental, 207.

Above, the Mark VI chassis as introduced in 1946, and below, the standard steel saloon of 1946–1952, Bentley's first venture into the field of coachbuilding, employing pressed steel construction, with all finishing of interior trim and paintwork being carried out in their own Crewe works. This edition later became known as the "small boot" model, to differentiate between the later larger boot 'R' Type.

Vanden Plas, before being absorbed into the B.M.C. empire to produce Princess limousines, for a short post-war period continued to construct specialist coachwork on Bentley chassis, and here we see all three different forms emerging from their long established Hendon works. The hard top and drop head coupé edition above sharing the same body panels below the waistline, while at the bottom, is the four door saloon, a similar body also being fitted to the large Austin of that time (1946.)

The Norfolk body building concern of Duncan emerged in the immediate post-war period as a new name in the coachbuilding industry, and on the left is their four seater drop head coupé offering.

Harold Radford's name has long been associated with the motor trade, and in 1947 his "Countryman" made its appearance, providing a luxury shooting brake positively bristling with gadgets, from picnic and cocktail sets to washing facilities and inbuilt grandstand for viewing point-to-point meetings.

His Royal Highness Prince Bernhard of the Netherlands himself designed this very special four seater drop head coupé, with a cowled front reminiscent of the Corniche of 1939/40, fitted to chassis number B311CD, and registered HX 13 NL.

With the Bentley company now producing their own coachwork on mass production lines, the days of the individual specialist coachbuilder were numbered, and Windovers, who produced this close coupled two door saloon, were not to survive as body-builders long after 1946.

A page devoted to the craft of Abbott, another coachbuilder whose days were numbered as constructors of their own designed bodies. Above is their 1951 drop head coupé, then a two light creation.

Above, an Abbott line evolved for the Continental model chassis, though also fitted to the more prosaic standard Mark VI chassis as well, while below, their drop head coupé for 1952 had now sprouted quarter lights behind the front door pillars, to afford additional viewing for the rear seat passengers.

This page is taken up with the craftsmanship of James Young, and above is their "Teardrop" sedanca coupé, the unusually shaped quarter windows lending a very individual line, as well as affording extra visibility.

If these special sedancas appear to have something in common with some Gurney Nutting styling, this could be accounted for as both these coachbuilding concerns were by then part of the Jack Barclay empire. Above, there is a hint of the Brougham by James Young of 1939, and the sedanca coupé, below, reflects much of Gurney Nutting's pre-war models.

Mr. O. F. Rivers, of Hoopers, had a series of specially cast silver crests in the pattern of the Maharajah of Mysore's coat of arms, for a series of cars supplied to this Indian potentate, a similar sedanca coupé to this was also supplied to the Regent of Iraq in 1949.

Below, is a Franay Sedanca Coupé on a 1951 chassis, number B182LLJ, belonging to that perfectionist collector, Jack Nethercutt, Esq., in California.

The second special H. J. Mulliner short razor edged saloon to be executed to the special design of R. G. McLeod (see page 220 for the first 4¼ Litre model). Their High Vision 'Perspex' panel in the roof again featured on this 1947 version.

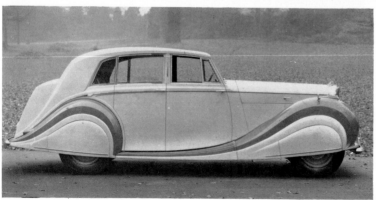

Above is the second edition of Harold Radford's Countryman, now coachbuilt with metal panels, in place of the earlier wooden shooting brake construction. With appropriate registration number HAR 1, this Monte Carlo Rally entry won a premier award in the specialised coachwork section. To the left is a Freestone and Webb special saloon with all enveloping mudguards.

For a brief time, there was an unhappy period for producing slab sided bodies, and here James Young, renowned for elegant coachwork, apparently succumbed to this modern trend.

Above, again James Young wrestled with the problem of blending this new form into an acceptable shape, though here their four door version met with but little additional success aesthetically. Whereas below, the slight break in mudguard line (if it can be called such) helped enormously in this more modern styling, being complemented with a cowl design of their own derivation.

James Young produced this style of saloon in both two and four door versions, then favouring the slightly flattened wheel arch form, popular at that time.

One of Hooper's prettiest offerings, which appeared as shown here, in two door form, as well as a four door model. This style was retained from 1951 until 1955.

Here, James Young wisely forsook the flattened wheel arches, as depicted in the car at the top, and achieved a nicer line as a result.

H. J. Mulliner still clung on to a distinct mudguard form in this well proportioned two door sports saloon. It is presumed the white walled tyres were a client's own personal preference.

Freestone and Webb also retained the old traditional mudguarding effect, though now an integral part of the coachwork, in this attractive two door saloon.

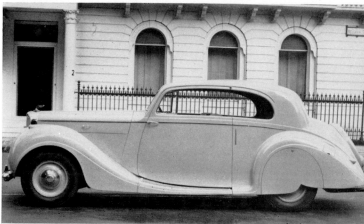

Another Freestone and Webb two door sports saloon, this time on a slightly earlier chassis and reproducing their pre-war semi-recessed rear spare wheel style as adopted by them in about 1935.

Here, a marked similarity can be noted in this James Young two door razor edged sports saloon to their 1939 prize winning design.

Messrs. Park Ward retained this design from about 1950 until 1955, in both fixed head (as shown here) and drop head forms. Their 1951 Motor Show stand displaying both versions in a striking colour scheme of silver grey and maroon.

Park Ward's development of their four seater drop head coupé throughout the period 1947–1955 is clearly shown here. The top car still retains the 1946 standard front mudguard shape, to later be swept back into the body sides, as displayed in the process of construction, and the final product. An electrically operated hood could be provided, and, unwisely, this could be operated while the car was in motion, a demonstration not to be encouraged.

No, surprisingly enough, these two convertibles are not by the same coachbuilder. The one depicted above is a rare edition from Messrs. Park Ward, dispensing with their usual rear quarter lights, while that shown below is by H. J. Mulliner, still offering its rear passengers that small added visibility in closed form.

James Young, who were
responsible for this four door
saloon, often used design
features closely resembling those
of H. J. Mulliner, both
concerns for so many years
producing some of the most
aesthetically satisfying creations
seen.

Here James Young show their
four door version of a style shown
on page 252. In those days each
body was hand crafted, before the
later cut and weld era.

Between about 1951 and 1954,
H. J. Mulliner produced a four
door saloon known as the
"Lightweight" model, and this
1952 version displays the slight
semi razor-edged treatment to the
rear head profile, which
contributed so much to the lines
of this edition.

Rippon Bros. were building
coaches long before the advent of
the motor car, and this four
door saloon was constructed by
them towards the end of their
lifetime as coachbuilders, as that
part of their activity ceased
in 1958.

This page depicts varying forms of the razor-edged styling by specialist coachbuilders. That at the top is by James Young, in four light form and perhaps a little heavy in appearance around the rear quarters.

Possibly one of the nicest and best balanced bodies of that time, is this by H. J. Mulliner, and one of their earlier special bodies on the Mark VI chassis. Excellent visibility is afforded and the whole presents a light pleasing appearance.

Hooper's version also employed small quarter lights brought back into the hood line, but failed to impart quite the panache of the car shown above.

Freestone and Webb's bodies could often be mistaken for H. J. Mulliner's work, and this model of theirs was a popular style retained for several years.

Another saloon by H. J. Mulliner showing this company's mastery of this styling. This edition is thought to be their 1951 model.

Facel-Metallon was the name used by the company producing this close coupled coupé, and the similarity between the French Facel Vega and this version will be apparent.

Above, another Continental close coupled coupé, this time by Farina, produced in June 1954, on the 'R' Type Continental chassis, and to the left, Saoutchik's exotic interpretation of a drop head coupé, reminiscent of Delahayes and Lago Talbots of that time (circa 1950).

Both these two door sports saloons are by Farina, the upper one displayed at the 1948 Paris Salon on the Bentley stand, and the lower one is their 1950 version, now with a neater and more dignified radiator grille.

Freestone and Webb would appear to have borrowed H. J. Mulliner's form for concealing the hood when folded down, in this drop head coupé of theirs, thought to be about 1951.

This drop head is a rather rare example emanating from Messrs. Hooper and Co. (Coachbuilders) Ltd., who appear to have mastered the difficulty of folding the hood cant rails very neatly here.

While here H. J. Mulliner have resorted to their old method of hiding the hood beneath one of their cleverly devised rear folding panels.

Freestone and Webb again, this time displaying a drop head coupé on an earlier chassis than that depicted at the top of this page, probably circa 1947.

Above, still bearing resemblance to their pre-war style, Gurney Nutting evolved this three position hood for their 1950 drop head coupé models, while below, Park Ward despatched this convertible model as part of a "Show the Flag" demonstration in the United States in 1947.

Hooper's retained this design between 1951 and 1955 for their razor-edged saloons and a well devised one, too.

Above, perhaps the form of the chromium waist line strip is the most obvious identification to distinguish between this H. J. Mulliner saloon and the Freestone and Webb version depicted below.

Hooper's stock of special silver crests were again in demand to equip this special four door saloon for H.H. Maharajah of Mysore in 1949, while below, Freestone and Webb in the sweeping lines displayed here, have acquired a little of the Hooper look.

H. J. Mulliner produced this special fast back sports saloon before the advent of their Continental model and apparently incorporated their 'Perspex' panels in roof.

Above is the 1951 prototype H. J. Mulliner Continental, with divided windscreen and one inch lower than the production models. Chassis number BC26A, registered OLG 490, and owned by Stanley Sedgwick, while to the left, James Young remodelled this H. J. Mulliner edition to present this form.

Above is the production Continental version, this one being the company's demonstration car, chassis number BC11C, registered SMA 410, and owned by Lawrence Dalton, while to the right, is another of R. G. McLeod's special designs evolved for him by H. J. Mulliner. Below, the Park Ward edition, of which only five were constructed for the 'R' Type Continental.

How specials materialise, above, Bob Gooda's conversion with spoiler rear, contrasting with the standard steel saloon 'R' Type, as shown below, and in which form this competition special probably first started life.

CHAPTER THIRTEEN

'S' SERIES

Though at first it was thought there would be little material available covering this model without resorting to some repetition, a little searching unearthed no less than 21 different forms of coachwork fitted to the three models, S I, S II and S III.

The first edition arrived late in 1955, and the engine bore very close resemblance to the previous 4.9 Litre 'R' Type, though the bodies, now of Rolls-Royce own manufacture, were entirely different, and the styling was so well conceived as to make the task of the specialist coachbuilder indeed a difficult one, in achieving any improvement upon its almost faultless lines.

With the introduction of the S II Series in 1959, Bentleys dropped the in-line six cylinder engine of 4,887 c.c., to replace it with an eight cylinder of 6,230 c.c., with a 90° V formation of General Motors design, the automatic transmission fitted to this model was also derived from the same source.

The S III Series in 1962 saw further transatlantic flavour with twin head lamps, and also the end of the special higher performance engine for the Continental model, it being felt that the maximum speed available from the standard machine, with compression ratio now raised to 9.8 to 1, gave all that modern motoring conditions demanded.

Brief Specification: **S I Series.** $3\frac{3}{4}$ in. bore $\times 4\frac{1}{2}$ in. stroke, 4,887 c.c.

Six cylinder push rod operated overhead inlet, side exhaust valve engine.

Wheelbase: 10 ft. 3 in. and 10 ft. 7 in.

Track: (Front) 4 ft. $8\frac{1}{2}$ in.

(Rear) 4 ft. $10\frac{1}{2}$ in.

Number of cars made: Standard chassis, 3,009

Long wheelbase chassis, 35

Continental, 431.

S II Series: 4.1 in. bore $\times 3.6$ in. stroke, 6,230 c.c.

90° V8 cylinder push rod operated overhead valve engine.

Chassis dimensions as S I Series.

No production figures yet available.

S III Series: As for S II series but with compression ratio increased to 9.8 to 1.

The standard steel saloon introduced in 1955 and continued throughout the three 'S' series Bentleys until the arrival of the 'T' in 1965. The beautifully balanced lines lent themselves to conversion to drop head form as devised by H. J. Mulliner, seen below, by retaining the main lower panel shapes throughout.

The end of an era, Hooper's swan song. Above, is Mr. Rivers' design for the Continental model, of which it is thought only five were made, this being their exhibit for the 1959 Earls Court show, and below, is H.H. the Maharajah of Bawalpar's saloon supplied in April 1956, on the standard 'S' chassis.

Park Ward, before their name became hyphenated with H.J. Mulliner, produced both hard top and convertible coachwork for the Continental chassis and their drop head version is shown here, a highly desirable motor for

Above, H. J. Mulliner here forsook the standard lines to produce this alternative version of a two door convertible model, while below, Park Ward changed their design from that shown on the previous page to concur with the "Graber" line, then fashionable.

With four seats and four doors, one can only evolve so much in the best of taste and still retain individuality. James Young made but few changes from the standard version in their saloon shown here.

Possibly it was thought that by spending some £10,000 on a highly desirable grand tourisme motor, one might expect more than two doors and folding front seats, so H. J. Mulliner produced the "Flying Spur", as shown here equipped with four doors.

A rather rare edition of the "Flying Spur", by H. J. Mulliner, this four door Continental model kept basically to a four light concept, and at the loss of a little vision possibly presented a more balanced appearance.

Perhaps the unbroken waist line is as good an identification as any in distinguishing the difference between the work of these two master craftsmen. This is James Young's interpretation for a four door Continental model saloon in 1963.

The life of individual coachbuilders is fast running out, and above, James Young present their own design, the four light sports saloon on the Continental of 1957–1958.

If you own one of these H. J. Mulliner special saloons on the standard 'S' series chassis, then you probably have one of three such creations. This one is Sam Shoup's pride and joy in Tennessee.
Though the 'S' series standard wheelbase was 11 ft. 3 in. a longer version with an extra four inches was also available. Below, James Young present a style more familiar with the Rolls-Royce cars, providing extra accommodation and more elaborate cabinet work.

H. J. Mulliner, for the 'S' series, still retained their familiar fast back style, but differentiated between the earlier edition by introducing scalloping into the rear mudguards, and also offered an alternative form as shown below, with a larger boot and raised rear roof line.

Above, James Young's version is distinguishable by that unbroken line picking out the mudguard contours, while on the left, H. J. Mulliner executed their fourth special body to R. G. McLeod's design incorporating their familiar perspex sun roof, with perhaps some Issigonis' leanings? Below, another James Young two door saloon, offering interesting contrast to the H. J. Mulliner coachwork on the opposite page.

1958, and those two great names in coachbuilding, *H. J. Mulliner* and *Park Ward*, had now become joined together as the originators of these two editions for the last of the distinctive Continental models, while the tuned engine still provided added performance over the standard 'S' series.

CHAPTER FOURTEEN

'T' SERIES

1969—Fifty years of Bentleys. Whatever historians record in the very eventful life of this famous marque, and particularly in those dramatic days of 1931, when the assets of the old company were so nearly acquired by Napiers, renowned for the excellence of their aero engines, their once Grand Prix winning motors and luxury machines—it cannot be denied that this esteemed name has lost nothing in its standing through its acquisition by Rolls-Royce.

Their latest creation, the 'T' Series, may have been heralded by some criticism of its possibly too "ordinaire" compact appearance, yet for utterly restful travel in present modern traffic conditions, I would venture to say it is still unsurpassed, considering the purpose for which it is designed.

Because of the nature of its construction employing the latest monocoque, chassis-less form, the degree of variety in coachwork is of necessity restricted. It still amazes me, considering both the time and considerable cost involved in producing the non-standard coachwork as emerging from H. J. Mulliner–Park Ward Ltd., that the queue of patient and discerning motorists who await delivery of their £11,101 worth of transportation, is the enormous length that it is.

To maintain the very highest standard is not easily done, and I for one am grateful that this superb product should come from Great Britain.

Brief Specification: 4.1 in. bore × 3.6 in. stroke, 6,230 c.c.
90° V8 cylinder push rod operated overhead valve engine.
Wheelbase: 9 ft. $11\frac{1}{2}$ in.
Track: (Front) 4 ft. $9\frac{1}{2}$ in.
                (Rear) 4 ft. $9\frac{1}{2}$ in.

Above, the 'T' Series in standard four door saloon form, and below, the H. J. Mulliner–Park Ward special two door version, the construction of which involves some to-ing and fro-ing between Crewe and London of various components, before the final product is finished off at the coachbuilder's premises to the exceptionally high standard that has become accepted as synonymous with these two great names.

For a very brief period, James Young produced an alternative form to the standard saloon by cutting out the four doors, and substituting two only, to present the form seen above, and below, the 1968 Paris Salon and later the Earls Court Motor Show, saw this special Pininfarina two door sports saloon displayed. This car may well become unique, as no series production is at present envisaged.

The company specially photographed this rare drop head coupé version by H. J. Mulliner–Park Ward, chassis number CBX6357, on 21st February 1969, prior to her leaving for the United States and her fortunate owner, so that I might accurately call this book, Fifty Years of the Marque. Similarity of line with the fixed head coupé version will be apparent and interior seating accommodation is also the same for both models. The hood in folded form presents this profile because concealment meant loss of luggage space and complication involving the rear suspension.

CHAPTER FIFTEEN

CREWE IN COMPETITION

The year 1969 is far removed from the days of 1934, when E. R. Hall, by means best known to himself, managed to gain the blessing of Messrs. Rolls-Royce Ltd. to his private entry of a $3\frac{1}{2}$ Litre Bentley in the Tourist Trophy Race. Previously no owner of a car emerging from this illustrious company's portals had ever disregarded their policy for complete abstention from all forms of motoring competition.

In the past, however, their Schneider Trophy successes not only had placed Great Britain in the forefront of aviation, but that same design had also provided the means for our gaining air supremacy over Hitler's Luftwaffe, and it is no exaggeration to say that to those Rolls-Royce engines many of us owe our very existence today.

The passing of more than twenty post-war years has brought a new type of Bentley into competition—the Crewe Special. Elderly Mark VI's, 'R' Types and even 'S' Series are being converted into low weight machines, of rather similar appearance, due to their basic design features, which can make the best Vintage Bentley breathe very heavily in a Silverstone blind, though I do feel the 'T' Series must surely present problems in modification to even such enterprising enthusiasts as the Bradley Brothers.

However, it is thought that some very special gearing will be called for, before the Ghent times fall to the lot of this modern brigade, but when heavy braking and ease of manoeuvrability are required they are indeed a force to be reckoned with. As Sotheby prices place our beloved everyday vintage transport in the spiralling realms of the antique business, these quite inexpensive racers, for which replacement engines are still available over the counter, do indeed offer a tempting alternative to those little tin boxes and beetles which so drearily litter the club circuits of today.

Unfortunately, not a team of 'R' Type Continental Bentleys entered for Le Mans, but a line up in front of the Cunningham pits in 1953 of the cars used by Walter Heaton, Bill Spear, Charles Faroux and Briggs Cunningham, while below are a few Continentals attending a rally at the Welcome Hotel, Stratford-on-Avon.

Bob Gooda's Special splashing round Silverstone in a club race, here, I believe, driven by Brian Dumps. Below, H. C. Green, a demonstrator at the 1964 Goodwood Pageant, in his "Flying Spur" Continental, finds an open section of the course to wind up the machinery, and enjoy himself.

Both these Mark VI specials were evolved by Major Jack Bailey, their creator here listed in the programme as driving No. 10, fighting it out with A. E. Padgett in No. 23, who presumably had now acquired LTU 951, while a member of the Vintage brigade presses gamely on in their wake.
It is in the tighter corners of the club circuits that these Crewe built "dicers" show off to some advantage over the cart sprung machines of an earlier decade.

The 'R/S' Type special built up by the Bradley brothers for W. R. Cheston, and then so superbly rebuilt by Douglas Symonds in his inimitable fashion, here to be presented at The Dorchester Hotel, showing how these machines can be turned out. Below, Mike Bradley, who with his brother Bob started it all, is about to make fastest time of the day at Firle Hill, with a 28.30 seconds climb in 1967.

A Silverstone line up of some of the chief exponents of this latest form of Bentley racing motor. From left to right, Major Jack Bailey, W. R. Cheston, Mike and Bob Bradley, ministering to their current edition, and Brian Shoosmith with his mount.

This scene depicts that delightfully informal and friendly atmosphere which members of the Bentley Drivers Club come to associate with their "raison d'être".

Throughout their entire existence, Bentleys have never been only just a means of transportation, they have become a way of life, and still a sporting challenge in this present day. "Bentley fifty years of the Marque"

INDEX

INDEX

INDEX

INDEX

INDEX

INDEX

INDEX